Write Away 3

Write Away 3

A Course for Writing English

Donald R. H. Byrd
Hunter College
CUNY Graduate School
The City University of New York

Gloria Gallingane
La Guardia Community College
The City University of New York

Newbury House Publishers, New York
A division of Harper & Row, Publishers, Inc.
Grand Rapids, Philadelphia, St. Louis, San Francisco
London, Singapore, Sydney, Tokyo

Director: Laurie E. Likoff
Production Coordinator: Cynthia Funkhouser
Text and Cover Design: Ron Newcomer
Text Illustrations: Carol Ann Gaffney and Anna Veltfort
Photo Research: Robin Risque
Production: R. David Newcomer Associates
Compositor: TypeLink, Inc.
Printer and Binder: Malloy Lithographing, Inc.

NEWBURY HOUSE PUBLISHERS
A division of Harper & Row, Publishers, Inc.

Language Science
Language Teaching
Language Learning

Write Away 3: A Course for Writing English

Library of Congress Cataloging-in-Publication Data

Byrd, Donald R. H.
  Write away: a course for writing English / Donald R. H. Byrd,
Gloria Gallingane.
      p.   cm.
    ISBN 0-06-041088-4 (v. 2).—ISBN 0-06-041089-2 (v. 3)
    1. English language—Textbooks for foreign speakers.   2. English
language—Rhetoric.   I. Gallingane, Gloria.   II. Title.
PE1128.B85   1990   89-13290
428.2′4—dc20   CIP

93 92 91 90   9 8 7 6 5 4 3 2 1

Acknowledgments

Working with other people sweetens the task of writing textbooks. *Write Away* is the result of a long collaboration that has been often tested. I am indebted to Gloria Gallingane for her abiding commitment to these materials, a commitment I shared. Seeing them so successfully used by teachers and students certainly helped to make our experience and theories about teaching writing real. The names of people I particularly wish to thank include: Effie Cochran, Rena Deutsch, Joan Dye, Nancy Frankfort, Cindy Funkhouser, Jack Gantzer, Nancy Gross, Jann Huizenga, Judy Gex, Laurie Likoff, Grace Martinez, Robert Miller, Ron Newcomer, Ann Raimes, Ken Sheppard, Rick Shur, Carolyn Sterling, Howard Stitzer, and Stanley Zelinski. Two people especially enrich and give purpose to my life: Sarah Henderson Byrd Flanagan and Athanassios Doumanidis. To them I lovingly dedicate this book.

Donald R. H. Byrd

Co-authors of texts develop their own *modus operandi* and this holds true for the two authors of this three-book *Write Away* series. In planning for the revision and expansion of the original two-book series into three, Dr. Donald R. H. Byrd and I decided that he would assume responsibility for Book 3, I would revise Book 2, and together we would recreate Book 1; a division of labor well-suited to our busy professional lives. Dr. Byrd is and has been an excellent role model as a textbook writer, indefatigable and creative, and I want to thank him first and foremost for his enthusiasm and dedication to this project. Thanks also to members of the editorial staff at Newbury House, and to Ron Newcomer, our West Coast editor, for their infinite patience. And sincere thanks to the following friends and colleagues who, through comments and suggestions, have directly influenced some of the units in this series: Pamela Breyer, Irene Dutra, Winifred Falcon, Gary Gabriel, Jean McConochie, and Ellen Shaw. Finally, this book is dedicated to the memory of James E. Weaver, whose teaching and materials inspired countless young and inexperienced ESL teachers and always impressed his colleagues. His untimely death in 1984 is still mourned by his many friends and former students.

Gloria Gallingane

Photo Credits

Contents

Introduction

Write Away is a three-book series for students of English. The series helps students write English better through an integrative four-skill approach and through specially designed guided-to-free exercises.

The three books progress in grammatical, lexical, and rhetorical difficulty either by isolating specific points for writing practice or by allowing students to experiment with various means of expression through sentence combinations.

The *Write Away* approach views writing, like other language skills, as the acquisition and mastery of various components ("isolates") that fit together as a whole in communication.

Written English, after all, is communication, and writing is a skill that connects with other language skills. In *Write Away* this connection is deliberately exploited. In fact, this holistic treatment is an integral part of the *Write Away* approach as revealed in the sequence of exercises. Although the exercises always lead to a well-formed composition, they treat more than just writing skills *per se*.

The topics in *Write Away* were chosen according to these general criteria: (1) the intrinsic interest of the content; (2) accurate reflection of the real world; (3) appropriateness to the students' needs; (4) potential for getting students to react; and (5) suitability to serve as a basis for language expansion. These topics, at times, entertain, inform, or gently provoke—but never offend or insult. Classroom piloting of the materials helped to eliminate undesirable topics. The students, therefore, should be allowed and encouraged to react orally through discussions and brainstorming before they write.

The Organization of *Write Away* Units

Students and teachers will quickly become familiar with the "friendly" layout of *Write Away*, the pleasant illustrations and airy design, the developmental sequence of exercises that lead to the end product, and the clear focus of the exercises.

The first exercises in each *Write Away* unit focus on vocabulary expansion and reading comprehension. The purpose of these exercises is to introduce the "access" vocabulary and the ideas needed for the subsequent writing practice. Access vocabulary refers to those pivotal words that are needed for a clear understanding and discussion of the topic, whether in speech or in writing. It is not surprising, then, that these new words are defined very specifically in the exercises—only as they are used in the unit. We opted for this streamlined treatment of word meaning because further dictionary colorings would only bewilder students at this stage.

The second skill that *Write Away* treats is reading. The reading exercises are receptive; that is, they do not require the students to produce any new information. Using tasks such as matching, multiple choice, fill-in, and sequencing, students are tested as to how well they understand the content of the unit. These exercises (exercise B) are called "Reading Preview," and they are positioned just before the model paragraph or the sentences to be combined (exercise C). Exercise D provides the focused writing activity.

Invariably students, through their own experience, will know something about the topic, and the initial exercises tap and expand that knowledge. The exercises are most effectively used by having the students, without the intrusion of the teacher, compare their answers to the exercises *before* and *after* they read. This comparison reveals, in a general way, students' progress in understanding the ideas and in recognizing the vocabulary in the unit.

Exercise D in each *Write Away* unit is the "core" writing activity—usually one of two task types: *rewriting* of a model composition (usually a paragraph); or *combining* short sentences that are parts of longer, natural-sounding stretches of discourse. As the writing exercises are laid out developmentally in a single unit, students are expected to use a mixture of rewriting and combining operations. These operations might be likened to various "revising" efforts, with the developed composition being the final result. *Write Away* anticipates what the end composition should look like and, through a choice of focused exercises, guides students through the processes that produce a well-formed composition.

Throughout the vocabulary, reading, and writing exercises, students are led through a sequence of tasks, from recognition to production. The first tasks of each unit are for recognition purposes only. They do two things: present access vocabulary intrinsic to the unit; and check the reading comprehension of the ideas contained in the unit. After students become familiar with the vocabulary and the content, they are ready to start the production tasks of writing.

Following all focused writing practice (through paragraph rewriting or sentence combining), there is a culminating free, individualized composition assignment (exercise E "Writing Follow-Up"). This composition is the moment of truth, for the entire value of the previously executed exercises in the unit are put to the test. The essential purpose of the previous practice was to prepare the students for this ultimate stage of composing. Predictably, the topics suggested for "Writing Follow-Up" are thematically, rhetorically, and grammatically related to the previous parts of the unit. Students, after the concentrated analysis and revision of the model composition, easily make the transition to composing on their own, going from analysis and manipulation to analogy. To ensure this transition, there are guided questions to encourage the students to put their own ideas on paper—either in class overseen by the teacher or as homework.

The Role of the Teacher in Using *Write Away*

Some roles a teacher or tutor may assume while using *Write Away* include these: *facilitator/expeditor* (making sure circumstances, reference materials, and classroom set-up are conducive to writing); *monitor* (being available to answer questions when solicited); *pacer* (keeping the students on task within time constraints); *nurturer* (making the students feel good about their own writing accomplishments); and *participant* (showing a personal interest in the students' ideas and ways of expression).

The design of the materials in *Write Away*, since they foster student autonomy, are easily used in all individualized learning situations, such as learning and literacy centers and, especially, in writing laboratories. Whether in the hands of an experienced or inexperienced teacher, a trained or untrained tutor, the exercises are easily used and are non-threatening. However, it is most important that the teacher or tutor not let the writing practice become tedious or tiresome. Vigilance is necessary to ensure that the focused writing practice does not become an end unto itself. An almost certain invitation to ennui is to treat the practice as methodical or routine. The writing exercises are seen as means to an end—not an end unto themselves. Their purpose is for students to end up with an acceptable, well-formed, cohesive composition.

Naturally the teacher, being the expert, must judge which practice activities the students need. The teacher also should decide on the kinds of activities for different students (since individual needs vary), how these activities are to be done (in pairs, in groups, with individuals, or as a whole class), and how much time to allow for the various sequences (most units should take no more than an hour or two, at most, excluding the homework assignment that follows).

Generally students like to talk about the ideas they encounter, and the judicious teacher will not only allow students to talk but will build in discussion activities in each class. This free—and certainly spontaneous—exchange of ideas allows students to practice their oral expression without the intrusion of grammatical and vocabulary rules. These times of expression also serve to humanize the writing class.

The *Write Away* System

The exercises in *Write Away* are grammatically focused and are always meaningfully contextualized. Students will be able to use their understanding of the content to sharpen their grammatical accuracy. The system developed for *Write Away* resulted from a unique analysis of the various grammatical operations that a writer utilizes when writing and revising. As stated earlier, the advantage of using *Write Away* is that these grammatical operations in writing and revising are anticipated and laid out in the sequence of each unit. The results of the operations applied in sequence will produce a well-formed composition.

There are a variety of ways to express oneself. *Write Away* has codified these ways, called operations, into four categories: (1) inflectional; (2) coordinative; (3) subordinative; and (4) derivational. Any well-formed composition contains a mixture of these grammatical operations. If any operation is faulty, it is distracting, sidetracking the reader from the *what* of expression to the *how*. These operations, then, are not seen as ends unto themselves. Rather, they should be seen as the means to the end of clear expression. They provide the *how* of expression so that the *what* of expression is clear.

(1) *Inflectional* writing operations are the most fundamental parts of English grammar. Inflectional endings are important elements

in standard English. The parts of speech in English that inflect are: nouns, verbs, adjectives and adverbs, and pronouns.

(2) *Coordinative* operations use such words as *and, but*, and *or*, and they serve to join equal elements together like single words (*boys and girls, he and she, blue and yellow*), phrases (*She dances and swims well, . . . out of sight and out of mind*), and clauses (*He danced with Mary, but he didn't dance with Helen*).

Coordinative operations are good ways to put short sentences and sentence parts together to form longer, more complex structural hierarchies. This way writers avoid short, unnatural staccato sentences that tire the reader. Coordinative operations, then, help to make one's writing smooth and flowing, and they, along with subordinative operations, frequently occur in the numerous sentence combining exercises in *Write Away*.

(3) *Subordinative* operations include the insertion of words or clauses that modify, describe, or amplify in some way different sentence parts: adjective words, phrases, or clauses that modify nouns; and adverb words, phrases, or clauses that modify verbs, adjectives, or other adverbs. Noun clauses are discussed below.

The simplest subordinative maneuver is the insertion of a single-word adjective or adverb as in these examples: *blue book*; *he ran quickly*. There are, of course, more complex subordinative operations, like the insertion of adjective phrases as in *that book on the desk* or the adverb phrases as in *He ran like a rabbit*.

The most complicated subordinative procedure occurs with clauses because of various reference, syntactic, or other concomitant grammatical considerations. Basically, there are two kinds of clausal subordination: adjective (relative) clauses (usually with *who(m)*, *that*, or *which*) and adverb clauses (using such subordinating conjunctions as *because, although, even though, since, while, when, as soon as, until*, and so on).

Noun clauses with *wh-* words (*What he said was regrettable*) or *that* (*It is regrettable that he said that*)—although they are not technically subordinative structures—are treated in *Write Away* as subordinative operations since they, like the subordinative structures above, are the product of the union of two elements, one of which is relegated to a dependent syntactic status. Noun clauses, like adjective and adverb clauses, share the characteristic of being dependent clauses. In the case of noun clauses, however, they form a higher level constituent that, like dependent clauses, needs the rest of the sentence. In other words, noun clauses, like adjective and adverb clauses, cannot stand alone isolated from the rest of the sentence.

(4) *Derivational* operations occur when one part of speech changes, usually through suffixation, to another part of speech. Such lexical derivations include changes from a verb to a noun (*teach/teacher*, *assist/assistant*), an adjective to a noun (*happy/happiness*, *true/truth*, *different/difference*), an adjective to an adverb (*extreme/extremely*), a noun to a verb (*analysis/analyze*, *mystery/mystify*), and from a noun to an adjective (*child/childish*, *hope/hopeful*). There are some derivational prefixes that occur in English as in *danger/endanger*, where the noun is changed to a verb.

A good dictionary is a valuable tool for students when they are unsure of the derivational contrasts of words. It is not sufficient merely to be aware of the different derivations of words in isolation; one also has to know how the derived forms are used in sentences. Learners need to know specifically which function words cluster with the different derivations. A complete learner's dictionary will show not only the different derivations of words but will also show through examples how these variations are used in stretches of language. For example, when using the different derivations of *interest*, the student also has to know that *in* follows the adjective *interested* as in the sentence, "I am *interested in* art" or that *to* follows the adjective *interesting* as in the sentence "Art is *interesting to* me."

To the Student

Every language has its own grammatical system. *Write Away* deals with the grammatical system of written English. In order to help students write better, *Write Away* uses a special approach based on our analysis of written English.

Certain operations recur in all written English sentences. In writing, as in speaking and other language skills, there is a variety of ways to say the same idea. In most cases, a fluent speaker may use any one or more of these ways to express the same idea.

Let's explore the various ways of rendering approximately the same meaning in various different grammatical ways. Look at the sentence below:

The Macedonians conquered the Persians in 331 B.C.

The underlying idea in this sentence can be stated in a number of ways without substantially changing its meaning, as follows:

1. Macedonia conquered Persia in 331 B.C.
2. . . . the Macedonian conquest of Persia in 331 B.C.
3. . . . Macedonia's conquest of Persia in 331 B.C.
4. The Persians were defeated by the Macedonians in 331 B.C.
5. Persia was defeated by Macedonia in 331 B.C.
6. . . . the Persian defeat by Macedonia in 331 B.C.
7. . . . Persia's defeat by Macedonia in 331 B.C.

The same information about what happened between Macedonia and Persia in 331 B.C. is generally revealed by using various inflectional and derivational variations.

In each sentence the same information is presented in a different manner, using different grammatical ways. In *Write Away*, there will be many opportunities to write sentences like these examples.

In *Write Away* there are vocabulary and reading exercises before the writing exercises. These exercises help you to become familiar with the new words and ideas in the unit. You will probably want to talk about the ideas with your classmates.

After you become familiar with the new words and ideas in each unit, it is time to practice writing. There are two kinds of writing exercises: rewriting a model composition, and sentence combining.

A Rewriting Example

Rewriting exercises involves writing a model paragraph according to a sequence of instructions. When you finish the last rewriting exercise, you will end up with a well-formed composition. Here is an example of a rewriting exercise.

Princess of Rock

(1) Princess is a famous rock singer. (2) She gives concerts all over the world. (3) Many young people want to be like her. (4) She makes a lot of money. (5) She owns a silver jet. (6) She flies it herself. (7) She lives like royalty. (8) She remembers her poor childhood in Chicago.

Here are some typical *Write Away* exercises for the above model paragraph.

1. Johnny Punk is a rock singer, too, but he is not like Princess. Write about him.

Your first sentence: **Johnny Punk isn't a famous rock singer.**

2.   Princess does not give concerts any more. She lives a quiet life in the country with her family. Write about her in the past.

Your first sentence: **Princess was a famous rock singer.**

3.   Princess's daughter Ruthie wants to be a rock singer like her mother when she grows up. Write about her in the future.

Your first sentence: **Ruthie is going to be a famous rock singer.**

4.   Rewrite the paragraph by combining the following sentences. Omit the numbers.

Combine (1) and (2) with **, who**.
Combine (3) and (4) with **because**.
Combine (5) and (6) with **, which**.

NOTE: Omit **it** in (6).

Combine (7) and (8) with **, but**.
In (8), change **her poor** to **the poverty of her**.

Exercise 1 practices certain grammatical points: the negative forms in the present tense, and the changes in nouns and pronouns from feminine to masculine. Exercise 2 focuses on the past tense endings. Exercise 3 treats the *going to* future with the auxiliary changes. These exercises give you grammatical practice of different points in meaningful situations. The whole writing activity comes together in exercise 4. This final rewriting results in a natural composition. You can see the use of various words (like *but, who, because, which*), and word changes (like *poor/poverty*) that make the paragraph smoother and easier to read. The paragraph on the next page is the result.

Princess of Rock

Princess is a famous rock singer, who gives concerts all over the world. Many young people want to be like her because she makes a lot of money. She owns a silver jet, which she flies herself. She lives like royalty, but she remembers the poverty of her childhood in Chicago.

A Sentence-Combining Example

The second kind of writing activity in *Write Away* allows you to express yourself in your own way. Sentence-combining activities require you to put smaller sentences together to form more complex sentences that are easier to read. Here is an example of a sentence-combining activity.

The Liberation of Mrs. Denis

1. a. Mr. Denis is a clerk.
    b. He works in a post office.

2. a. He always eats dinner.
    b. He always eats it as soon as he gets home.

3. a. One day he came home.
    b. He was tired.
    c. He was hungry.
    d. His dinner was not ready.

4. a. Mrs. Denis was reading a book.
    b. The book was about women.
    c. It was about their liberation.

5. a. Mr. Denis got angry.
    b. He said that he was going to a restaurant.
    c. He was going there to eat.

6. a. Mrs. Denis asked him to be patient for a few minutes.
    b. She left the room.

7. a. He thought that she went to prepare dinner.
    b. After a few minutes she appeared.
    c. She was wearing her hat.
    d. She was wearing her coat.
    e. She was wearing her gloves.

8. a. She smiled.
    b. Her smile was sweet.
    c. She said, "I'm ready, dear. Where are we going to eat?"

In a sentence-combining activity, like the one above, you can combine the sentences in more than one way. For example, you can combine 1a and 1b in a number of ways, such as:

1. Mr. Denis is a post office clerk.
2. Mr. Denis is a clerk in a post office.
3. Mr. Denis is a clerk, who works in a post office.
4. Mr. Denis, a clerk, works in a post office.

The finished sentence-combining activity would look something like the following:

The Liberation of Mrs. Denis

Mr. Denis is a post office clerk. He always eats dinner as soon as he gets home. One day he came home, tired and hungry, but dinner was not ready. Mrs. Denis was reading a book about women's liberation. Mr. Denis got angry and said he was going to a restaurant to eat. Mrs. Denis asked him to be patient for a few minutes and left the room. He thought that she went to prepare dinner, but after a few minutes she appeared, wearing her hat, coat, and gloves. She smiled sweetly and said, "I'm ready, dear. Where are we going to eat?"

After you finish a sentence-combining activity, always check your work to see if the way you combined the sentences is natural sounding. You can check your work with the Answer Key, which the teacher has, or the teacher may check your work with you. In either case, the Answer Key shows the most natural combinations as written by native speakers. Not every possibility is in the Answer Key, however. If your combinations are different, check with your teacher.

We hope the exercises in *Write Away* help you improve your written English along with your other English skills. We also hope you have a pleasurable experience using *Write Away*. Now get out your paper and pen, and . . . *Write Away*.

Unit 1

Kitchen Kutters for Sale

A. Vocabulary Preview

These words occur in Part C. Match each word with its
definition. (You have to use one letter three times.)

_g_	1. gather around	a. small
_b_	2. kutter*	b. cutter, knife
_h_	3. demonstrate	c. cut in some way
_c_	4. chop	d. immediately
_c_	5. slice	e. There you are!
_c_	6. shreds	f. long, narrow pieces
_a_	7. tiny	g. come near
_d_	8. instantly	h. show
_e_	9. Presto!	
_f_	10. strips	

B. Reading Preview

Read the paragraph in Part C and then answer these
questions:

1. In (5), what does **them** refer to?
2. In (7), what does **them** refer to?
3. In (9), what does **it** refer to?

*This is not the spelling in the dictionary. The correct spelling is
cutter. Sometimes companies change the spelling of a word to
make the name of their product easy to remember.

4. In (11), what does **it** refer to?
5. Which vegetables does the Kitchen Kutter cut?
6. What does the machine do to onions? To tomatoes? To a head of cabbage? To a cucumber? To a carrot? To her finger?

C. Read the following:

Kitchen Kutters for Sale

(1) Gather around this table, ladies and gentlemen. (2) My name is Priscilla. (3) I'm going to demonstrate this machine, the Kitchen Kutter. (4) Do you see these onions? (5) This machine chops them into little pieces. (6) Do you see these tomatoes? (7) This machine slices them quickly and evenly. (8) Do you see this head of cabbage? (9) This machine shreds it into tiny pieces instantly. (10) And this cucumber? (11) This cutter turns it into these thin slices. (12) Now, look at this carrot. (13) Presto! This machine turns it into this pile of strips. (14) Oh! I cut my finger. (15) As you see, ladies and gentlemen, this Kitchen Kutter cuts everything!

D. Write Away

1. You are Priscilla's helper. Rewrite the paragraph.

Your first three sentences:

1. **Gather around that table, ladies and gentlemen.**
2. **Her name is Priscilla.**
3. **She's going to demonstrate that machine, the Kitchen Kutter.**

2.   Insert the following *adjectives* in the sentences indicated.

In (3), **fantastic**

Your first sentence: **I'm going to demonstrate this fantastic machine, the Kitchen Kutter.**

In (5), **wonderful**
In (7), **efficient**
In (9), **incredible**
In (11), **amazing**
In (13), **marvelous**
In (15), **convenient**

3.   Insert the following *adverbs* before the adjectives you've inserted in the sentences in exercise 2.

In (3), **absolutely**

Your first sentence: **I'm going to demonstrate this absolutely fantastic machine.**

In (5), **incredibly**
In (7), **extraordinarily**
In (9), **truly**
In (11), **positively**
In (13), **extremely**
In (15), **fantastically**

4.   Write five sentences that will help to sell the Kitchen Kutter. Use a word from column 1 and column 2 in each sentence.

EXAMPLE: This Kitchen Kutter is incredibly simple.

Adverb	Adjective
incredibly	simple
extraordinarily	efficient
extremely	convenient
fantastically	helpful
marvelously	beautiful
unbelievably	cheap
wonderfully	reasonable
positively	inexpensive
amazingly	modern
truly	good-looking

E. Writing Follow-Up

Are you a good salesperson? In the space below, write a
sales speech for a household item. Use expressions similar
to those in exercise 4.

_____

_____

_____

_____

_____

_____

_____

_____

_____

Unit 2

Retirement

A. Vocabulary Preview

Circle the one word or phrase that is different in each group. Explain why it is different.

1. (read)   play (tennis)   hike

2. read   write   (paint)

3. take (college courses)   read   (travel)

4. golf   tennis   (novel)

5. (travel)   hike   paint

6. play (golf)   (read)   grow

B. Reading Preview

Read the information in Part C and then answer the question about each person's retirement plans. Who plans to do:

athletic activities?
artistic activities?
intellectual activities?
relaxing activities?

C. Read the following:

Retirement

The people on the following page belong to the same social club. They are all ready to retire from their jobs.

Person	Retirement plans
1. Luigi	catch up on his reading
2. Chang	play tennis and golf
3. Pedro	grow orchids
4. Stella	travel in the Orient
5. Yolanda	take college courses
6. Ruth	paint portraits of her family and friends
7. Aaron	write a novel
8. Herman	hike across the country

D. Write Away

1.   Tell what each person plans to do.

Your first sentence: **Luigi plans to read.**

2.   Tell how each person plans to spend his time.

Your first sentence: **Luigi plans to spend his time reading.**

3.   Tell what each person plans to do, beginning with the word **What**.

Your first sentence: **What Luigi plans to do is read.**

4.   Rewrite each sentence in exercise 3 using the sentence below as a model.

Your first sentence: **Reading is what Luigi plans to do.**

E.   Writing Follow-Up

Everybody makes plans for retirement. Complete this paragraph about your father's or mother's or someone else's retirement plans.

My Father's (or Mother's) Retirement

My father plans to retire. (*When?*) _When he will 65year old_. After retirement, he hopes to _go on to a long trip to deffient countries_ because _he wants to spend time with my mom_.

He likes to _spend time with my mom_ because _she is the most important_ person in _his life and he is very happy when he spends for wonderful moments together with her._

Now write about your own retirement plans.

                My Retirement
        I plan to retire when I'll be
    have 65 years old. When that
    day comes I want to be with my
    husband still and with my Grandchildren.
    I want a big second wedding.
    Also a big honeymoon alone
    with my husband. It is great
    I love it .

Unit 3

Inflation

A. Vocabulary Preview

Find the words in Part C that mean:

1. _____ to change (lifestyles)

2. _____ become (angry and sad)

3. _____ can't find (jobs)

4. _____ without courage

5. _____ not happy

6. _____ feel pain

7. _____ old people's retirement money

8. _____ not enough

9. _____ ought to

B. Reading Preview

Inflation causes which of the following? Read the paragraph in Part C and then circle your answers.

Yes   No   1. A change in people's lifestyles?

Yes   No   2. A decrease in unemployment?

Yes   No   3. Anger and depression by workers?

Yes   No   4. Shortages of food for families?

Yes   No   5. Low-paying jobs for young people?

Yes   No   6. Food and rent increases?

Yes   No   7. Government inactivity?

Yes   No   8. Suffering by old people?

C.   Read the following:

Inflation

(1) Inflation causes people to alter their lifestyles. (2) Workers lose their jobs. (3) They get angry and depressed. (4) It is difficult for parents to buy all the necessary food for their families. (5) Young people are unable to find jobs. (6) They become discouraged and unhappy. (7) Old people suffer the most. (8) Their monthly pension checks are insufficient to pay for their food, rent, clothing, and medical expenses. (9) They feel that the government should do something about the high cost of living.

D.   Write Away

Inflation

1.   Rewrite the paragraph, but write about *one person only*.

people = a person
workers = a worker
parents = a parent
they = he or *she*

Your first sentence: **Inflation causes a person to change his or her lifestyle.**

2.   Rewrite the model paragraph in the *past tense*.

Your first sentence: **Last year inflation caused people to change their lifestyles.**

3.   Rewrite the paragraph, but change the time by adding **For the last several years** to the first sentence.

Your first sentence: **For the last several years, inflation has caused people to change their lifestyles.**

4.   Rewrite the model paragraph by inserting the following words in the sentences. Omit the numbers.

In (1), **usually**
In (2), **often**
In (3), **gradually**
In (4), **always**
In (5), **frequently**
In (6), **slowly**
In (7), **generally**
In (8), insert **seldom**; change **insufficient** to **sufficient**
In (9), **strongly**

E.   Writing Follow-Up

Write a report about some economic problems in your country. Mention how these economic problems affect lifestyles, job situations, cost of living, and pensions.

_____

_____

_____

_____

_____

_____

_____

_____

_____

Unit 4

Teeth: Early Weapons

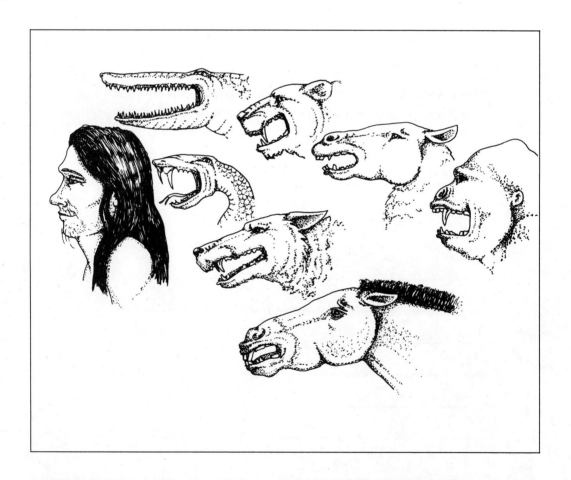

A. Vocabulary Preview

There words occur in Part C. Match each word with its definition.

_____   1. tools

_____   2. weapons

_____   3. survived

_____   4. defend

_____   5. enemies

_____   6. primarily

_____   7. teeth grinding

_____   8. instinct

_____   9. protect

_____ 10. ancestors

_____ 11. sharp

a. cutting easily
b. mainly
c. natural behavior
d. rubbing one's teeth together
e. instruments for fighting
f. people related to you from long ago
g. to keep safe from harm by covering
h. to keep safe from harm by fighting back
i. instruments for work
j. remained alive
k. people who wish to hurt you

B. Reading Preview

Read the sentences in Part C. Then say if these statements are _True, False, Probably,_ or _Not Likely._

1. _____ The ancestors' teeth were sharp.

2. _____ Our ancestors had a lot of hair.

3. _____ Early humans needed their teeth as weapons.

4. _____ They killed with their teeth.

5. _____ They also had metal weapons.

6. _____ The women also needed their teeth to kill.

7. _____ The women protected their throats with their hair.

8. _____ When people sleep, they dream of weapons.

9. _____ Humans' instincts are to protect each other.

10. _____ Women and young children do not fight.

C. Read the following:

Teeth: Early Weapons

1. a. Our early ancestors began to make tools.
   b. They began millions of years ago.
   c. They probably used their teeth as weapons.

NOTE: Use **Before** before 1a.

2. a. Some scientists believe early humans survived.
   b. They used their teeth.
   c. They used them to kill their enemies.

NOTE: Use **because** before 2b.

3. a.   In fact, early humans probably defended themselves.
   b.   They did this primarily with their teeth.

4. a.   At the same time nature gave males a beard.
   b.   The beard was thick.
   c.   The beard protected their throat.
   d.   The protection was against the bites.
   e.   The bites were of their enemies.

5. a.   Today a strong man can kill another man.
   b.   He can kill him with just a single bite.
   c.   The bite is on the throat.
   d.   Modern males rarely use their teeth.
   e.   They fight.

NOTE: Use **but** before 5d and **when** before 5e.

6. a.   By comparison, however, women bite.
   b.   By comparison, however, young children bite.
   c.   They are not very strong.
   d.   Their biting is frequent.
   e.   They fight.

NOTE: Use **when** before 6e.

7. a.   When sleeping, many people grind their teeth.
   b.   This teeth grinding is perhaps related to early humans' instincts.
   c.   The instinct is to protect themselves.
   d.   Their protection is by keeping their weapons sharp.

D.   Write Away

On your own paper combine the sentences in Part C. Write each group as one sentence.

E.   Writing Follow-Up

Write a paragraph about some of the weapons that people use today. How do people use these weapons? Are they necessary?

_____

_____

_____

_____

_____

_____

_____

_____

Unit 5

A Beautiful Bridge of Death

A. Vocabulary Preview

Find the words in Part C that mean:

1. _____ a bridge suspended by heavy metal ropes.

2. _____ to kill oneself.

3. _____ opinion that others have about something (or someone)

4. _____ serious, sad

5. _____ happened

6. _____ something that blocks the way

7. _____ keeping, maintaining

8. _____ having beautiful form, proportions

9. _____ causing great excitement, thrilling

10. _____ to make a great effort

B. Reading Preview

Read the sentences in Part C. Then cross out the one answer that is *not* true, according to the story.

1. The Golden Gate Bridge is (famous, beautiful, dangerous).

2. It is famous for its (beauty, tragic reputation, engineering).

3. Many people (enjoy, jump off, build barriers on) the bridge.

4. Some people object to (the bridge,   the barrier,   the suicides).

5. A barrier would probably (destroy the beautiful view, decrease the number of suicides,   be difficult to build).

6. The number of suicides from the bridge (is greater than from any other bridge,   has increased since 1937,   has decreased since the barrier).

C. Read the following:

A Beautiful Bridge of Death

1. a. The Golden Gate Bridge is a beautiful bridge.
   b. It is a suspension bridge.
   c. It is in San Francisco.

2. a. It is very famous for its beauty.
   b. It is very famous for something else.

NOTE: Use **as well as**.

3. a. Many people jump off this bridge.
   b. These people want to commit suicide.

4. a. The bridge opened in 1937.
   b. Hundreds of people have committed suicide.
   c. The suicides were by jumping off it.

NOTE: Use **Since** before 4a and **,** after 4a.

5. a.   According to news reports, the bridge has a reputation.
    b.   Its reputation is tragic.
    c.   More suicides have occurred there than any other place in the world.

NOTE: Use **because** before 5c.

6. a.   Engineers want to build a barrier.
    b.   The barrier is to prevent suicides.
    c.   The suicides are in the future.

7. a.   However, they are concerned.
    b.   Their concern is about preserving the beauty.
    c.   The beauty is graceful.
    d.   The beauty is of the bridge.
    e.   Their concern is about preserving the view.
    f.   Their view is spectacular.

8. a.   Engineers struggle with the problems.
    b.   The problems are of preventing suicides.
    c.   The problems are of preserving the bridge's beauty.
    d.   Most people continue to enjoy the bridge.
    e.   A few people still use it to commit suicide.

NOTE: Use **As** before 8a and , after 8c. Use **while** before 8e.

D. Write Away

Combine the sentences in Part C. Write each group as one sentence.

E.   Writing Follow-Up

Write a description for a travel brochure about a beautiful place in your country, such as a bridge, a building, a monument, a statue, or a park.

_____

_____

_____

_____

_____

_____

_____

_____

Unit 6

Flying Ghosts

A. Vocabulary Preview

1.   These words appear in Part C. Match each word with its definition.

_____   1. crash

_____   2. circulate

_____   3. crew

_____   4. versions

_____   5. haunted

_____   6. source

_____   7. proof

_____   8. ghost

_____   9. pilot

a. having ghosts
b. evidence that something is true
c. people who work in a plane
d. a dead person who appears again
e. a violent plane accident (noun) or to have a violent plane accident (verb)
f. different accounts of an event
g. origin, starting point
h. pass from one person to another
i. the person who guides a plane or ship (noun) or to guide a plane or ship (verb)

2.   Fill in the missing words in the chart below. You can find these words in Part C. Then, write the number(s) of the sentence where you find the missing word.

Verb	Which lines?	Noun	Which lines?
to _____	3a	crash	4a
to _____	_____	pilot	_____
to _____	_____	flight	_____
to prove	_____	_____	_____
to step	_____	_____	_____
to attend	_____	_____	_____

B. Reading Preview

Read the sentences in Part C and then number the order of these events.

_____ a. The crew and some passengers died.

_____ b. There were many versions of the ghost stories.

_____ c. Other crews told stories of seeing the ghosts of the dead crew.

_____ d. The company says there is no proof that the ghosts exist.

_____ e. The airline company made an investigation.

_____ f. A plane crashed at an international airport.

C. Read the following:

Flying Ghosts

1. a. Some pilots believe a story.
    b. Some flight attendants believe a story.
    c. This story is strange.

2. a. There are ghosts.
    b. They are on some jet planes.
    c. The jet planes belong to an airline.
    d. The airline is well known.

3. a. A few years ago, one of its jets crashed.
    b. It crashed in a field.
    c. The field was near an international airport.

4. a. The pilot died in that crash.
    b. Other crew members died in that crash.
    c. Some passengers died in that crash.

5.   a.   Now, other pilots see the faces.
     b.   Now, flight attendants see the faces.
     c.   The faces are of the pilot and crew members.
     d.   They died in that crash.

6.   a.   These faces appear on other jet planes.
     b.   Some pilots are afraid.
     c.   Some flight attendants are afraid.
     d.   They are afraid to fly over the area of the crash.

7.   a.   There are ten or twenty versions of the story.
     b.   The story is about the haunted jets.
     c.   Officials of the airline cannot find the source of
          the story.

8.   a.   They have talked to flight crews.
     b.   They have checked flight records.
     c.   They have taken other steps.
     d.   The steps are to get the facts.

9.   a.   As a result, officials of the airline say there is
          no proof at all.
     b.   The proof is that ghosts exist.
     c.   They exist on their jets.
     d.   Reports of the ghosts continue to circulate.

10. a.   Some people hear this story of the haunted jets.
     b.   They remember the story of *The Flying
          Dutchman.*
     c.   *The Flying Dutchman* is an opera about a dead
          sailor.
     d.   He had to pilot his ship forever.

NOTE: Use **When** before 10a.

D. Write Away

Combine the sentences in Part C. Write each group as one sentence.

E. Writing Follow-Up

1. Go to the library and read any information you can find about Richard Wagner's opera, *The Flying Dutch-man*. Summarize the information in a paragraph of no more than ten sentences.

2. Do you know a ghost story, perhaps about a haunted house or a dead person who reappeared? Write the story.

_____

_____

_____

_____

_____

_____

_____

_____

Unit 7

A Devilish Film

A. Vocabulary Preview

Match the exclamation with the situation.

_____ 1. Disgusting!

_____ 2. Exciting!

_____ 3. Shocking!

_____ 4. Boring!

_____ 5. Terrifying!

_____ 6. Frightening!

_____ 7. Disappointing!

_____ 8. Amazing!

_____ 9. Amusing!

a. listening to a dull speaker who goes on and on
b. hearing a funny joke
c. seeing a ghost
d. watching a good soccer match
e. being in an earthquake
f. hearing a quiet person use foul language
g. the fact that an ant can carry four times its own weight
h. learning that you didn't pass an exam
i. seeing something unpleasant that makes you sick

B. Reading Preview

Read the following paragraph. Then write another word that means the same as the italicized word(s). Use these words: _disappointing violence boring plot movie heroine humor surprising dialogue frighten_

Last Saturday we went to see a   (1) *moving picture*, one of these   (2) *slow-moving* tragedies, where the (3) *female hero* dies at the end. The   (4) *conversation* was especially uninteresting. The   (5) *story line* fascinated us, however, because it combined a lot of   (6) *fighting* with (7) *amusement*. The suspense did not really   (8) *scare* us and the special effects were not particularly   (9) *unexpected*. Overall, it was kind of   (10) *less than what I hoped for*.

C. Read the following:

Here are some comments from people who saw the movie *The Devil's Delight*.

A Devilish Film

(1)   "Fascinating Plot"

(2)   "Frightening Suspense"

(3)   "Shocking Special Effects"

(4)   "Exciting Acting"

(5)   "The ending was terrifying."

(6)   "All the violence was disgusting."

(7)   "The humorous scenes were amusing."

(8)   "The actors were annoying."

(9)   "The dialogue was interesting."

(10) "The slow scenes were boring."

(11) "The background music was amazing."

(12) "One disappointing development was the death of the heroine."

D.   Write Away

1.   Practice asking and answering questions with a classmate. Then, write questions and short answers.

Your first sentence: **What was fascinating? The plot was.**

2.   Jessica and Hannah saw the movie. Write about their feelings, using information from exercise 1 above.

Your first sentence: **Jessica and Hannah thought the plot was fascinating.**

NOTE: In (2) through (10), use **They**.

3.   Rewrite the sentences in exercise 3, using the sample below as a model.

Your first sentence: **The plot fascinated them.**

E.   Writing Follow-Up

Write a review of a movie that you saw. Tell the title of the movie and what you thought of the plot, the music, the acting, the beginning and ending, the dialogue, and the special effects.

_____

_____

_____

_____

Unit 8

The International Sport

A.   Vocabulary Preview

Circle the one word that is different in each group. Explain why it is different.

1. boring   satisfying   exciting   exhilarating

2. frustrating   thrilling   disappointing   boring

3. witnessing   observing   watching   being

4. match   game   action   player

5. skill   lose   action   speed

6. never   sometimes   always   usually

B.   Reading Preview

Complete these sentences. Use these words: *excites   disappointed   boring   fascinated   thrilling   satisfaction*

1. "I really feel _____ . My favorite team lost 3 to 1."

2. "It's so _____ . Tonight's game will decide the winner."

3. "What really _____ me is seeing two good teams go at each other."

4. "I'm _____ by the action of the game."

5. "I get so much _____ out of observing the skill of the teams."

6. "It's never _____ to me when it all happens so fast."

C. Read the following:

The International Sport

(1) Attending a soccer match is never boring. (2) On the contrary, seeing two teams compete is usually exciting. (3) Following the action of the game is particularly fascinating. (4) Also, witnessing the speed of the players is exhilarating. (5) Observing the skill of both teams is satisfying. (6) Yet, watching a favorite team lose is always disappointing. (7) At such times being a spectator is sometimes frustrating. (8) However, watching an important soccer game is invariably thrilling.

D. Write Away

1.   Tell a friend about soccer. Begin each sentence with **It is . . . to . . .**

Your first sentence: **It is never boring to attend a soccer match.**

2.   Eugenia is a serious basketball fan. Write about her.

Your first sentence: **Attending a basketball game never bores Eugenia.**

3.   Rewrite the sentences you wrote in exercise 2 and describe Eugenia's feelings.

Your first sentence: **Eugenia is never bored attending a match.**

NOTE: In sentences (2) through (7), use **She.**

4.   Rewrite the paragraph by following the directions below. Omit the numbers.

Omit **Attending** in (1).
Insert **It is . . . to . . .** in (2). (See exercise 1 for example.)
Combine (3), (4), and (5) with **, and**. Omit **Also** in (4).
Insert **It is . . . to . . .** in (6). (See exercise 1 for example.)
Combine (6) with (7), using **, and**.
Do not change (8).

E.   Writing Follow-Up

Write about the most popular team sport in your country.
By answering these questions, you can create your
paragraph:

What is your favorite team sport?
Where do you play it and in which season?
What do you like particularly about this sport?
Who are some of the famous players, and what are they like?
*What do you like most about this sport, and do you think
    most other people like it for the same reason?*

_____

_____

_____

_____

_____

_____

_____

_____

Unit 9
Reading, Writing, and Arithmetic

A.   Vocabulary Preview

Write the word(s) that mean the following. Use these words:
*environment   look forward to   consider   appreciate
avoid   kindergarten   hurt one's feelings*

1.   _____   a school for pre-school children

2.   _____   come to a conclusion after much
                       thought

3.   _____   surroundings

4.   _____   keep away from

5.   _____   make someone feel mental pain

6.   _____   understand and enjoy the benefits of

7.   _____   anticipate

B.   Reading Preview

Read the paragraph in Part C and match the following:

_____	1. What does Bruce like?	a. being with them
_____	2. What does he consider rewarding?	b. watching them learn
_____	3. What does he enjoy?	c. numbers and letters
_____	4. What does he introduce his students to?	d. learning in pleasant surroundings
_____	5. What do they practice?	e. hurting their feelings
		f. seeing Bruce

_____	6. What does he encourage?	g. being Bruce's students
_____	7. What does he avoid?	h. teaching kindergarten
_____	8. What do the students appreciate?	i. counting and spelling
_____	9. What do they look forward to?	j. teaching young children
_____	10. What does he enjoy with his family?	

C. Read the following:

Reading, Writing, and Arithmetic

(1) Bruce likes teaching kindergarten. (2) He considers teaching young children very rewarding. (3) He particularly enjoys watching them learn. (4) He likes introducing young students to the world of numbers and letters. (5) His students practice counting things in the classroom. (6) Also, they practice spelling one another's names and objects in the room. (7) Bruce encourages learning in a pleasant environment. (8) He avoids hurting his students' feelings when they make mistakes. (9) His students appreciate being in his classroom. (10) They look forward to seeing him. (11) When he finishes teaching for the day, he enjoys going home and being with his family.

D. Write Away

1.   Bruce has a second job in a special government program, where he teaches adults how to read and write. Rewrite the paragraph to describe what *adult* classes are like.

Your first sentence: **Bruce likes teaching adults in the government program.**

2.   Natalie also teaches kindergarten, but she doesn't like to teach children. She is studying for a degree to teach university students. Write about her.

Your first sentence: **Natalie does not (doesn't) like teaching kindergarten.**

NOTE: In (6) omit **Also** and add **either** at the end of the sentence. In (11) do not add **doesn't**, but change **home and being with his family** to **to the university and taking evening classes**.

3.   Write short answers for these questions:

(1)   What does Bruce like?

Your first sentence: **Teaching kindergarten.**

(2)   What does he consider rewarding?
(3)   What does he particularly enjoy?
(4)   What does he like?
(5)   What do his students practice?
(6)   What does Bruce encourage?
(7)   What does he avoid?
(8)   What do his students appreciate?
(9)   What do they look forward to?
(10)   What does he enjoy when he finishes teaching?

4.   Use your short answers in exercise 3 to complete the following sentences.

(1) . . . **is what Bruce likes**.

Your first sentence: **Teaching kindergarten is what Bruce likes.**

(2) . . . **is very rewarding to him**.
(3) . . . **is particularly enjoyable to him**.
(4) . . . **is what he likes**.
(5) . . . **is what his students practice**.
(6) . . . **is what they also practice**.
(7) . . . **is what Bruce encourages**.
(8) . . . **is what he avoids**.
(9) . . . **is what his students look forward to**.
(10) . . . **is what they look forward to**.
(11) . . . **are what he enjoys when he finishes teaching**.

5.   Rewrite the model paragraph by following the directions below. Omit the numbers.

Combine (1) and (2) with **because**.
Combine (3) and (4) with **and**.

NOTE: Omit **He** in (4).

Combine (5) and (6) with **and**.

NOTE: In (6), omit **Also, they practice**.

Combine (7) and (8).

NOTE: Put **Since** before (7).

Combine (9) and (10) with **, and**.
Do not change (11).

E.   Writing Follow-Up

Write about your favorite teacher by answering these
questions:

Who is/was (s)he?
What does/did (s)he teach?
Which school does/did (s)he teach in?
How does/did (s)he conduct the class?
What kind of person is/was (s)he?
Why do/did you like her/him?
Where is (s)he now?
What would you say if you saw her/him?

_____

_____

_____

_____

_____

_____

_____

_____

Unit 10
City Living

A. Vocabulary Preview

1.   Find and write in the correct ending for each word in the left column. (You will have to make some spelling changes.) Then, match each word to its definition. Check your answers when you read Part C.

_____ 1. enjoy_____   *some*   a. some activity that relieves or entertains

_____ 2. education_____   *ly*   b. showing the characteristics of one kind or type

_____ 3. trouble_____   *y*   c. pleasant

_____ 4. occur_____   *ence*   d. causing a training of the mind

_____ 5. type_____   *ity*   e. movement, action, state of being active

_____ 6. health_____   *ion*   f. causing anxiety or trouble

_____ 7. active_____   *al*   g. in an unchanging, fixed manner

_____ 8. diverse_____   *able*   h. happening, event

_____ 9. constant_____   *ical*   i. state of being well

2.   Circle the one word that is different in each group.

1.   chore   task   occurrence

2.   diversion   pastime   feeling

3.   enjoyable   troublesome   annoying

4.   experience   feeling   occurrence

B. Reading Preview

Read the paragraph in Part C. Then tell what you think is *best* about living in a large city. Rank them with numbers. Discuss your answers.

_____ a. many exciting things to do

_____ b. many museums for educational growth

_____ c. a lot of concerts to enjoy

_____ d. opportunities to meet new people

_____ e. a mixture of international groups (neighborhoods, restaurants, etc.)

What do you think is *worst* about living in a large city? Rank them with numbers. Discuss your answers.

_____ a. the subways and buses

_____ b. pushing and shoving during rush hours

_____ c. dirty air and pollution

_____ d. occasional feelings of loneliness

_____ e. the amount of crime

C. Reading the following:

City Living

(1) Living in New York is exciting.   (2) Finding many things to do is always easy in the large city. (3) Visiting different museums is educational. (4) Attending concerts is enjoyable.   (5) Constantly meeting new people is interesting.   (6) Furthermore, observing different people from all over the world is fascinating.

(7) However, living in the Big Apple is sometimes annoying.   (8) Certainly, breathing the dirty air is unhealthy.   (9) Riding the subways and buses is often troublesome.   (10) Getting from one place to another is tiring and time-consuming at certain times of day.   (11) Being pushed and shoved is typical during rush hours. (12) Also, being on guard against crime is usual, particularly at night.   (13) Being alone occasionally in New York is not uncommon.   (14) Yet, being bored is very unusual.

D.   Write Away

1.   Rewrite the passage. Start each sentence with **It is**.

Your first sentence: **It is exciting to live in New York City.**

2.   Make the following changes in the model paragraph. Add **a** or **an** when necessary.

Add **experience** to (1).
Add **task** to (2).
Add **activity** to (3).
Add **diversion** to (4).
Add **experience** to (5).
Add **pastime** to (6).
Change **annoying** to **nuisance** in (7).
Add **practice** in (8).
Change **troublesome** to **problem** in (9).
Add **chore** to (10).
Add **occurrence** to (11).
Add **worry** in (12).
Add **situation** to (13).
Add **feeling** to (14).

3.   After you have made the changes in exercise 2, re-write the passage. Begin each sentence with **It is.**

Your first sentence: **It is an exciting experience to live in New York City.**

4.   Rewrite the model paragraph by following the directions below. Omit the numbers.

Insert **an . . . experience** in (1). (See exercise 2 for example.)
Begin (2) with **It is**. (See exercise 1 for example.)
Combine (3) and (4) with **, and**.
Do not change (5).
In (6) use **it is** after **Furthermore**. (See exercise 1 for example.)
Do not change (7) and (8).
Combine (9) and (10) with **, and**.
Begin (11) with **It is . . . occurrence**. (See exercise 3 for example.)
Add **you have to** and omit **is usual** in (12).
Do not change (13) and (14).

E.   Writing Follow-Up

In a letter to a pen pal, describe life in your own city. Mention in the first paragraph what is:

exciting to do
educational to do
enjoyable to do
interesting to do

Also, in the second paragraph, mention what is:

annoying to do
troublesome to do
time-consuming to do
unhealthy to do

————————————————
your street

————————————————
your city

————————————————
date

———————————————— ,
salutation

——————————————————————————

——————————————————————————

——————————————————————————

——————————————————————————

——————————————————————————

——————————————————————————

—————————————————————————— .

———————————————— ,
complimentary close

————————————————
your name

Unit 11

Country Living

A. Vocabulary Preview

Find and write in the correct ending for each word in the left column. (You will have to make some spelling changes.) Then match each word with its definition. Check your answers when you read Part C.

_____ 1. please	*ment*	a.	unusually good
	ant	b.	to one's liking;
_____ 2. peace	*ful*		sharing the
	able		same feeling
_____ 3. entertain	*ly*	c.	specifically
	action	d.	giving enjoy-
_____ 4. particular			ment to the
			senses
_____ 5. wonder		e.	in the same
			amount
_____ 6. agree		f.	amusement
		g.	contentment;
_____ 7. equal			pleasure
		h.	quiet, serene,
_____ 8. satisfy			untroubled

B. Reading Preview

Read the paragraph in Part C. Then say what you think is *best* about living in the country. Rank them with numbers. Put an X for the ones *not* typical of country living.

_____ a. peaceful nights for sleeping

_____ b. having a garden

_____ c. many kinds of entertainment

_____ d. fresh, clean air

_____ e. getting up early (to the alarm-clock call of a rooster)

_____ f. being close to nature

_____ g. going to bed early (to the lullaby of a night-ingale)

_____ h. noisy, polluted environment

C. Read the following:

Country Living

(1) It is so wonderful to live in the country.   (2) It is very agreeable to be close to nature.   (3) It is especially peaceful to go to sleep at night to the lullaby of a night-ingale.   (4) It is equally pleasant to wake up each morning to the alarm-clock call of a rooster.   (5) Furthermore, it is particularly healthy to breathe the fresh country air. (6) It is such a satisfaction to have a garden and watch the plants grow.   (7) It is also rewarding to grow most of your own food.   (8) Sometimes, it is boring not to have many kinds of entertainment.   (9) However, it is easy to appreciate the peace and quiet.

D. Write Away

1.   Living in the country is wonderful to Clara. Use the information in the model paragraph, and write about her feelings.

Your first sentence: **Living in the country is so wonderful to Clara.**

NOTE: In (2) through (9) change **to Clara** to **to her**.

2.   Write what Clara thinks about country living.

In (1), use **Clara thinks (that)** . . . .

Your first sentence: **Clara thinks (that) living in the country is so wonderful.**

In (2), use **She finds (that)** . . . .
In (3), use **She thinks (that)** . . . .
In (4), use **She feels (that)** . . . .
In (5), use **She agrees (that)** . . . .
In (6), use **She says (that)** . . . .
In (7), use **She agrees (that)** . . . .
In (8), use **She admits (that)** . . . .
In (9), use **She concludes (that)** . . . .

3.   Edgar has just moved to the country. He did *not* know the pleasures of country living. Rewrite that paragraph to describe what he did not know about country living. Use the information below.

In (1), use **Edgar didn't know that** . . . .

Your first sentence: **Edgar didn't know (that) it was so wonderful to live in the country.**

In (2), use **He was surprised (that)** . . . .
In (3), use **He was relieved (that)** . . . .
In (4), use **He discovered (that)** . . . .
In (5), use **Furthermore, he learned (that)** . . . .
In (6), use **He couldn't believe (that)** . . . .
In (7), use **Sometimes, he admitted (that)** . . . .
In (8), use **He agreed (that)** . . . .
In (9), use **However, he insisted (that)** . . . .

4.   Rewrite the paragraph you wrote in exercise 1. Insert *such a . . .* and the following words.

In (1), **way of life.**

Your first sentence: **Living in the country is such a wonderful way of life.**

In (2), **experience** (omit **very**)
In (3), **feeling** (omit **especially**)
In (4), **sensation** (omit **equally**)
In (5), **advantage** (omit **particularly**)
In (6), **activity**
In (7), **pastime**
In (8), **existence**
In (9), **thing**

5.   Rewrite the model paragraph by following the directions below. Omit the numbers.

Omit **so** in (1).
Use **being** in (2).
Combine (3) and (4) with **, and**.
Do not change (5).
Combine (6) and (7) with **, and**.

NOTE: In (6), change **and** to **to**. In (7), omit **It is also rewarding.** Add commas.

Combine (8) and (9) with **, but**.

NOTE: Omit **However**.

E.   Writing Follow-Up

Write a travel article about life in the country in your country. Mention what you find:

peaceful
healthy
rewarding
pleasant
satisfying

Also, mention what you find *boring* or *uninteresting*.

_____

_____

_____

_____

_____

_____

_____

_____

Unit 12

Nightingale
of the Nile

A. Vocabulary Preview

These words appear in Part C. Match each word with its definition.

_____ 1. harmony

_____ 2. rhythm

_____ 3. verse

_____ 4. Koran

_____ 5. overwhelming

_____ 6. thrilled

_____ 7. clapping

_____ 8. lasted

_____ 9. fans

_____ 10. finely tuned

_____ 11. nightingale

_____ 12. Nile

a. continued
b. section of poetry or song
c. adjusted to produce a nice sound
d. very powerful
e. people who love a performer
f. hitting hands together to show approval
g. regular repetition of a beat
h. a songbird
i. the holy book for Muslims
j. combination of musical notes
k. a river in Egypt
l. excited

B. Reading Preview

Read the sentences in Part C. Then describe whether these are _True (T)_ or _False (F)_. Circle the correct letter.

T   F   1. Egyptian music is similar to Eastern music.

T   F   2. Umm Kalthum used to sing religious verse.

T   F   3. She was born in Cairo.

T   F   4. Her fans thought her singing style was boring.

T   F   5. Her technique was to invent different harmonies.

T   F   6. Her concerts were usually short.

T   F   7. She also sang Western music.

T   F   8. Her singing had an emotional impact on her fans.

C.   Read the following:

Nightingale of the Nile

1. a.   Music is a language.
    b.   The language is international.
    c.   The music has its own character.
    d.   The character changes from country to country.

2. a.   Westerners notice the character of Arab music.
    b.   They notice it immediately.
    c.   The character is unique.
    d.   Arab music has different harmonies.
    e.   Arab music has different rhythms.
    f.   These harmonies and rhythms are different from Western music.

3. a.   The greatest singer of Arab music was Umm Kalthum.
    b.   She was Egyptian.

4. a.   She was born into a poor family.
    b.   The family lived in the Nile Delta.
    c.   There she started her career.
    d.   The start of her career was by singing verses.
    e.   The verses were from the Koran.
    f.   The Koran is the holy book for Muslims.

5. a.   Later in Cairo she improved her singing style.
    b.   Her style became strong.
    c.   Her style became emotional.
    d.   Her style became overwhelming.

6. a.   She developed a technique.
    b.   The technique was remarkable.
    c.   The technique involved repeating the same line.
    d.   The repetition was over and over again.

7. a.   During one concert she sang a single line.
    b.   She sang it in 52 ways.
    c.   The ways were different.

8. a.   Her voice thrilled her fans.
    b.   Her voice was unusual.
    c.   Her singing style thrilled her fans.
    d.   The fans reacted by screaming.
    e.   The fans reacted by crying.
    f.   The fans reacted by clapping.

9. a.   Thousands of men attended her concerts.
    b.   Thousands of women attended her concerts.
    c.   Thousands of children attended her concerts.
    d.   Her concerts often lasted six to eight hours.

10. a.   Her fans will remember her.
    b.   The memory will be for a long time.
    c.   It will be because of her voice.
    d.   Her voice was extraordinary.

e.   Her voice was like a musical instrument.
f.   The instrument was finely tuned.
g.   Her voice was well-suited to express the tones of
     Arab music.

D.   Write Away

Combine the sentences in Part C. Write each group as one
sentence.

E.   Writing Follow-Up

Write an article about your favorite singer. Mention:

who that person is
that person's background
how (s)he looks
how (s)he dresses
the kind of music (s)he sings
the way (s)he performs
a typical concert

_____

_____

_____

_____

_____

_____

_____

_____

Unit 13

What Happened to Sir Reginald?

A.   Vocabulary Preview

These words appear in Part C. Match each word with its definition.

_____   1. spy

_____   2. widely publicized

_____   3. agents

_____   4. assassinate

_____   5. espionage

_____   6. locked

a. closed and secured with a key

b. a person who tries to learn the secrets of another country

c. kill for political reasons

d. people who do secret or dangerous missions

e. well-known

f. the practice of spying

B.   Reading Preview

Read the sentences in Part C and then circle the correct answer:

1.   Sir Reginald was *not* (British,   an agent,   on an assignment).

2.   He was (50,   60,   63) years old when he disappeared.

3.   The discovery of the body embarrassed (his wife, his son,   the police,   his dogs)

4. He seemed peaceful because he was (with his dogs,

in his favorite chair,   locked in his library).

5. His body was found (three years after his disappear-

ance,   ten years after his retirement,

during World War II).

6. (His wife,   the police,   his son,   his dogs) found

the body.

C.   Read the following:

What Happened to Sir Reginald?

1. a.   Sir Reginald disappeared from his London
       home.
    b.   He was a spy.
    c.   He was British.
    d.   He disappeared one fall day.

2. a.   His son found his body three years later.
    b.   His disappearance was a mystery.
    c.   The mystery was widely publicized.

NOTE: Before 2a, use **Until**.

3. a.   Sir Reginald had many assignments in World
       War II.
    b.   These assignments were dangerous.
    c.   His most dangerous activities were in the Medi-
       terranean area.

NOTE: Before 3a, use **Although**.

4. a.   He worked in that area.
    b.   Agents tried to kill him.
    c.   These agents were foreign.
    d.   They did this three times.

NOTE: Use **When** before 4a.

5. a.   However, he was clever.
    b.   He always escaped the attempts.
    c.   The attempts were to assassinate him.

NOTE: Put **so** before **clever** in 5a and **that** before 5b.

6. a.   Sir Reginald announced his retirement.
    b.   He retired from espionage activities.
    c.   He did this when he was 50 years old.
    d.   His family did not believe him.

NOTE: Before 6a, use **Although**.

7. a.   Therefore, no one was surprised.
    b.   He disappeared suddenly.
    c.   It was after ten years of retirement.

NOTE: Before 7b, use **when**.

8. a.   Yet, three years later everyone was surprised.
    b.   His body was found.
    c.   It was found in a locked room.
    d.   The room was on the second floor.
    e.   The second floor was in his London home.

NOTE: Before 8b, use **when**.

9. a. The discovery of Sir Reginald's body embar-
      rassed the police.
   b. The body was in his own house.
   c. They had been careless in their search.

NOTE: Use **because** before 9c.

10. a. Sir Reginald, on the other hand, seemed at
       peace.
    b. He was sitting in his armchair.
    c. The armchair was his favorite.
    d. The armchair was in his library.
    e. It was locked.

11. a. His body was found.
    b. A mystery still remains.

NOTE: Before 11a, use **Although**.

12. a. How is it possible?
    b. His wife did not find him.
    c. His son did not find him.
    d. His dogs did not find him.

NOTE: Use **that** before 12b.

D. Write Away

Combine the sentences in Part C. Write each group as a
single sentence.

E.   Writing Follow-Up

Do you know of a mystery? Write the story. Tell:

why the story is a mystery
what happened
where/when it happened
who was involved

_____

_____

_____

_____

_____

_____

_____

_____

Unit 14

A Future Flying Fossil

A. Vocabulary Preview

These words appear in Part C. Match each word with its
definition.

_____   1. fossil

_____   2. escape hatch

_____   3. blinded

_____   4. glacier

_____   5. injured

_____   6. damaged

_____   7. peaks

_____   8. plateau

_____   9. sealed capsule

_____ 10. probe

a. flat mountaintop
b. a tightly closed
   metal container
c. an ice mountain that
   slowly moves
d. hurt or wounded for
   a person or animal
e. search deeply under
   or inside
f. a realistic formation
   in a rock over many
   years
g. not in working
   condition
h. caused to lose
   visibility
i. doors for emergency
   exit
j. pointed mountain
   tops

B. Reading Preview

Read the sentences in Part C and then circle the correct answer:

1. The DC-3 was flying from (Austria,   France,   Switzerland) to (Austria,   France,   Switzerland).

2. There were (8,   4,   12) people aboard the plane.

3. The plane crashed because of (pilot injury,   bad weather,   high mountains).

4. The plane did *not* crash in (a snowstorm,   the mountains,   France).

5. The plane was (on a peak,   on a flat mountaintop,   badly damaged).

6. The people were rescued (immediately,   after a few days,   two weeks later).

7. The Swiss did *not* (cover the plane with snow,   place a capsule inside the plane,   locate the plane under the snow).

8. The purpose of the capsule was to (give directions to the location of the plane,   to explain how the plane got there,   to honor the people in the crash).

C. Read the following:

A Future Flying Fossil

1. a. The DC-3 was an airplane.
    b. It was used during World War II.
    c. Its use was extensive.
    d. Few of these planes are in good condition today.

2. a. However, in Switzerland one exists in perfect condition.
    b. It exists because of an event.
    c. The event was unusual.
    d. It occured in 1946.

3. a. On November 19, 1946, a DC-3 took off from Vienna, Austria.
    b. It took off with eight passengers.
    c. It took off with four crew members.
    d. It was on its way to Istres, France.

4. a. The plane was flying over Switzerland.
    b. It ran into dark snow clouds.
    c. The clouds blinded the pilot.

NOTE: Use **As** before 4a.

5. a. A strong wind shook the plane.
    b. The shaking was violent.
    c. Then, the plane dropped like a stone toward earth.

6. a. The plane crashed in the Swiss Alps.
    b. No one was seriously injured.
    c. The plane was hardly damaged.

NOTE: Use **Although** before 6a.

7. a. The weather cleared up.
    b. Search planes located the DC-3.
    c. It was among the mountain peaks.
    d. It was resting on the only plateau within many miles.

NOTE: Use **After** before 7a.

8. a. The rescuers saw the plane from the air.
    b. They could not rescue the people immediately.

NOTE: Use **Even though** before 8a.

9. a. The passengers and crew members were rescued a few days later.
    b. Heavy snowstorms covered the whole Alpine region.

NOTE: Use **After** before 9a.

10. a. Pilots flew over the crash site two weeks later.
    b. They saw no trace of the plane.
    c. It was covered by snow.

NOTE: Use **When** before 10a and **because** before 10c.

11. a. Spring of 1947 came.
    b. The Swiss mountaineers climbed back to the plateau.
    c. They located the plane.
    d. They located it by probing through the snow.
    e. They probed with long poles.

NOTE: Use **When** before 11a.

12. a. They opened the escape hatch in the top of the cockpit.
     b. They did this by digging through the snow.

13. a. Inside the cockpit they placed a sealed capsule.
     b. In this capsule were copies of magazines.
     c. In this capsule were copies of newspapers.
     d. In this capsule were copies of photos.
     e. These magazines, newspapers, and photos told the story of the crash.
     f. Then they closed the hatch.

14. a. The Swiss placed the capsule in the plane.
     b. They knew the plane was sealed in a glacier.
     c. The glacier was slowly moving downhill.

NOTE: Use **because** before 14b.

15. a. Six hundred years from now, the plane will emerge.
     b. It will emerge from the ice.
     c. It will be ready to fly.

D. Write Away

Combine the sentences in Part C. Write each group as a single sentence.

E.   Writing Follow-Up

Do you know of an adventure story like this? Write the story. Tell:

why the story was an adventure
what happened
where/when it happened
who was involved
what the ending was

_____

_____

_____

_____

_____

_____

_____

_____

Unit 15
Some Elephant Surprises

A. Vocabulary Preview

These words appear in Part C. Match each word with its definition.

_____	1. remarkable	a. warm-blooded animals
_____	2. magnificent	b. natural, inborn feelings
_____	3. dense	c. thick
_____	4. dominated by a matriarch	d. groups of large animals
_____	5. herds	e. led by an older female
_____	6. patriarchal	f. large and handsome
_____	7. instincts	g. noteworthy
_____	8. mammal	h. led by an older male

B. Reading Preview

Read the sentences in Part C. Then describe whether these statements are *True (T)* or *False (F)*. Circle the correct letter.

T   F   1. Most elephant leaders are male.

T   F   2. Elephants prefer jungle environments.

T   F   3. All elephants live in family units.

T   F   4. Each elephant has his/her own personality.

T   F   5. Most of this information about elephants is new.

T   F   6. The size of an elephant's brain is about the same as a human's.

T   F   7. Most elephants behave according to instincts.

T   F   8. Elephants are afraid of humans.

C. Read the following:

Some Elephant Surprises

1. a. Animal researchers have made discoveries about elephants' behavior.
   b. The discoveries are remarkable.
   c. This has happened during the past decade.

2. a. They observed the African elephant.
   b. The African elephant is magnificent.
   c. It is the largest land animal in the world.
   d. It is one of the most advanced mammals on earth.
   e. It is advanced socially.

3. a. They found out that elephants can adapt to many environments.
   b. The environments are different.
   c. The environments include grasslands.
   d. The grasslands are flat.
   e. The environments include forests.
   f. The forests are dense.
   g. The forests are tropical.
   h. The environments even include mountain slopes.
   i. The slopes are cold.

4. a. They knew, of course, that elephants live in family units.
   b. These family units are stable.
   c. These family units are not dominated by a male but by a female.
   d. That female is called a matriarch.
   e. The matriarch is related to every other member of the family.

NOTE: Use **; however**, before 4c.

5. a. The matriarch is usually the mother.
   b. The matriarch is usually the grandmother.
   c. The matriarch is usually the sister.
   d. The matriarch is usually the aunt.

6. a. Until recently most animal observers thought that elephant herds were patriarchal.
   b. That is, the herds were led by male elephants.
   c. The males were old.
   d. The males were wise.

7. a. However, most male elephants leave the family unit.
   b. They do this when they are 10 to 13 years old.
   c. The matriarch pushes them out.

NOTE: Use **because** before 7c.

8. a. Actually the males live like bachelors.
   b. The bachelors are lonely.
   c. They join family units.
   d. They do this temporarily.
   e. They do this for mating purposes.

9. a.   Elephant watchers have observed something
         else about elephants.
    b.   Each elephant has a personality.
    c.   Its personality is distinct.

NOTE: Use : after 9a.

10. a.   In one family, for example, two elephants were
         always together.
    b.   They were female.
    c.   They were probably sisters.
    d.   They behaved quite differently.

11. a.   One was very curious.
    b.   She was unafraid of humans.
    c.   The other was shy.
    d.   She was afraid of humans.

12. a.   Like a human infant, baby elephants are born
         with a brain.
    b.   The brain is small.
    c.   The brain grows until adulthood.

13. a.   Their brain develops slowly.
    b.   Their behavior is not shaped completely by
         instincts.
    c.   Their personality is not shaped completely by
         instincts.
    d.   Their behavior is shaped mostly by the experi-
         ence of the family.
    e.   Their personality is shaped mostly by the expe-
         rience of the family.
    f.   They are also shaped by the teachings of the
         family.

NOTE: Use **because** before 13a.

14. a.   It is evident, then.
     b.   Elephants are intelligent.
     c.   Their behavior is complex.
     d.   Both of these characteristics are more than
          most people realized.

NOTE: Use **more** in 14b and 14c.

D. Write Away

Combine the sentences in Part C. Write each group as a
single sentence.

E. Writing Follow-Up

Answer the following questions. Pretend you are an ob-
server of humans. Write your answers in complete sentences to form one paragraph.

*What do we know about the intelligence and behavior of
    humans?*
What kinds of personalities do they have?
Where can they live?
What is the family unit like?
Who is the head?
How do the male and female humans live?

How do they act? How do they dress?
What are some of the discoveries about human behavior?

_____

_____

_____

_____

_____

_____

_____

_____

_____

Unit 16
Gypsies

A.   Vocabulary Preview

These words appear in Part C. Match each word with its definition.

_____   1. nomadic tradition

_____   2. migrated

_____   3. scattered

_____   4. concentration camps

_____   5. mistreat

_____   6. traders

_____   7. obstacles

_____   8. intervention

a. moved from one place to another to live

b. people who buy and sell items/objects as a way to make a living

c. abuse, deal with cruelly

d. barriers, walls that separate people

e. in many different directions

f. moving from place to place as a customary way of life

g. the act of taking control

h. places for prisoners of war

B.   Reading Preview

Read the sentences in Part C. Then cross out the word or expression that is not mentioned or that is incorrect.

1. Gypsies are (dark,   European,   nomadic) people.

2. Gypsies make a living by (telling fortunes,   trading, traveling).

3. The first gypsies came to Europe (over a 1000 years ago,   around A.D. 1100,   between 100 and A.D. 1100).

4. Hitler hated their (color,   way of life,   nomadic nature).

5. Recently governments have required them to (settle down,   go to school,   stop telling fortunes).

6. The benefits of settling down include (better health, tighter family ties,   more schooling).

C. Read the following:

Gypsies

1. a. Gypsies are people.
   b. They are nomadic.
   c. They live in all parts of the world.

2. a. Gypsy men make their living as metal workers.
   b. They make their living as auto mechanics.
   c. They make their living as traders.

3. a. Gypsy women are famous.
   b. Their fame is as fortune-tellers.

4. a. The first gypsies came from northwest India.
   b. They migrated to Persia.
   c. The migration was between A.D. 100 and A.D. 1000.

5. a.   In Persia they separated.
    b.   The separation was into different groups.
    c.   These groups still exist today.

6. a.   These groups scattered.
    b.   The scattering was throughout the world.

7. a.   Gypsies arrived in North America.
    b.   Their arrival was in the late 1800s.

8. a.   Many people do not like gypsies.
    b.   Many governments mistreat them.

9. a.   Hitler hated their dark skin.
    b.   He hated their way of life.

10. a.   He put them in concentration camps.
     b.   He sent them to the gas chambers.
     c.   Half a million gypsies died.
     d.   This happened between 1939 and 1945.

NOTE: Use **, where** after 10b.

11. a.   In order to stop the gypsies from traveling,
         some nations require them to register.
     b.   They require them to go to school.
     c.   They require them to learn trades.

12. a.   For example, in 1956 the Soviet Union passed a
         law.
     b.   The law required the gypsy groups to settle
         down.
     c.   They had to settle down in a place of their
         choice.

13.   a.   Obstacles such as mountains, deserts, and oceans never stopped the gypsies.
      b.   The obstacles were geographic.
      c.   Political walls between nations will bring an end to their nomadic tradition.
      d.   The walls are recent.
      e.   The end is almost certain.

14.   a.   The traveling of the gypsies may stop.
      b.   The cause is government intervention.
      c.   They will have more opportunities for better education.
      d.   They will have more opportunities for better health care.
      e.   Their living conditions will improve.
      f.   All these things are certain.

NOTE: Use **Although** before 14a.

D.   Write Away

Combine the sentences in Part C. Write each group as a single sentence.

E.   Writing Follow-Up

In most countries, there are unusual groups of people like the gypsies. Write a paragraph about those people. Talk about:

their origins
their occupations

their customs and traditions
their difficulties
their joys and pleasures
the changes in their lifestyle
the outlook for their future

Unit 17
Sister Serena

A.   Vocabulary Preview

Using prefixes, change these expressions into single words.

"not satisfied" _____ "not responsible" _____

"not organized" _____ "not secure" _____

B.   Reading Preview

Read the paragraph about Sister Serena. Then connect the answers to the questions.

a.   What does she try to solve?

b.   What is Sister Serena?

c.   What is a problem some people have?

d.   Why do people go to Sister Serena?

an advisor

personal problems for help

insecurity

C.   Read the following:

Sister Serena

Sister Serena is an advisor. Some people believe that she can solve any personal problem. Here are some questions that she usually asks people who come to her for help.

(1) *Are you unhappy?*
(2) *Are you unenthusiastic?*
(3) *Are you unpopular?*
(4) *Are you insecure?*
(5) *Are you inefficient?*
(6) *Are you irresponsible?*
(7) *Are you discontented?*
(8) *Are you dissatisfied?*
(9) *Are you disorganized?*

D. Write Away

1.   Sister Serena has many answers to the questions above. Look at her answers below and write in the missing nouns.

Your first sentence: **Sister Serena can reveal the secret of happiness to you.**

(2)   Sister Serena can fill you with _____.

(3)   She can increase your _____.

(4)   She can show you the way to _____.

(5)   She can help you become a model of _____.

(6)   She can develop a sense of _____ in you.

(7)   She can give you _____.

(8)   She can guarantee you _____.

(9)   She can put _____ in your life.

2.   Combine the questions in the model passage and the answers in exercise 1 with *If.*

Your first sentence: **If you are unhappy, Sister Serena can reveal the secret of happiness.**

3.   Imagine that someone did not have the problems above, but if (s)he had had these problems, Sister Serena *could have helped* him/her. Rewrite the sentences in exercise 2.

Your first sentence: **If you had been unhappy, Sister Serena could have revealed the secret of happiness.**

4.   Tell your imaginary friend that (s)he cannot hide his/her problems from Sister Serena. She knows *how* (s)he

feels. Write sentences using the adjectives in the model passage.

Your first sentence: **Sister Serena knows how unhappy you are.**

NOTE: Use **She** in (2) through (9).

5.   Now tell your friend that Sister Serena knows *why* (s)he has problems. Write sentences using the adjectives in the model passage.

Your first sentence: **Sister Serena knows why you are unhappy.**

NOTE: Use **She** in (2) through (9).

E.   Writing Follow-Up

Do you know someone like Sister Serena? How does that person help people? Write a paragraph about that person. Use the name of that person as the title of your paragraph.

_____

_____

_____

_____

_____

_____

_____

_____

Unit 18

Making Ends Meet

A. Vocabulary Preview

These words appear in Part C. Match each word with its definition.

_____ 1. deal with

_____ 2. budget

_____ 3. income

_____ 4. sacrifice

_____ 5. charity

_____ 6. interest rate

_____ 7. make ends meet

_____ 8. wise

a. earn enough money to pay expenses
b. money received from work
c. organization to help poor or needy people
d. percentage of money paid for borrowing money
e. plan one's money for living expenses
f. having good judgment
g. manage, live with
h. the act of doing without something that is needed or wanted

B. Reading Preview

Read the paragraph in Part C and check what people do to deal with inflation.

_____ a. They borrow money.

_____ b. They make sacrifices.

_____ c. They prepare budgets for their income.

_____ d. They buy more expensive items.

_____ e. They are careful about what they buy to eat.

_____ f. They give more money to charities.

C. Read the following:

Making Ends Meet

(1) Inflation is a serious economic problem for everybody. (2) Working people deal with it in a number of ways. (3) They budget their incomes carefully. (4) They buy cheaper kinds of meat, fruit, and vegetables. (5) They don't buy as many luxury items, such as cars. (6) They spend less money on travel and vacations. (7) They give less money to charities. (8) They don't borrow money from banks because interest rates are high. (9) In order to make ends meet, working people make many sacrifices. (10) They suffer along with everybody else.

D. Write Away

1.   Felipe is a hairdresser. Rewrite the paragraph. Tell about *his* problem.

Your first two sentences:

1. **Inflation is a serious economic problem for Felipe.**
2. **He deals with it in a number of ways.**

2.   Right now, middle-class people are having economic problems. Rewrite the paragraph. Write about *their* problems.

Your first two sentences:

1. **Inflation is a serious economic problem for middle-class people.**
2. **They're dealing with it in a number of ways.**

3.   Ten years ago, many people had economic problems. Rewrite the paragraph. Write about their problems *then*.

Your first sentence: **Ten years ago, inflation was a serious economic problem for everybody.**

4.   Insert the following expressions in the model paragraph.

In (2), **It's necessary for . . . .**

Your first two sentences:

1. **Inflation is a serious economic problem for everybody.**
2. **It's necessary for working people to deal with it in a number of ways.**

In (3), **It's important for . . . .**
In (4), **It's wise for . . . .**
In (5), **It's sensible for . . . .**
In (6), **It's common for . . . .**
In (7), **It's not unusual for . . . .**
In (8), **It's natural for . . . .**
In (9), **It's normal for . . . .**

NOTE: Insert after the comma.

In (10), change **They** to **Working people**.

E. Writing Follow-Up

Your answers to the questions below will form a paragraph. Write complete answers.

1. Why are you saving money (to buy new clothes, a car, a house or apartment, to pay for your education, to go on a vacation)?

2. How do you save money? (Many of the ways are mentioned in "Making Ends Meet.") Write at least *three* ways.

Saving Money

_____

_____

_____

_____

_____

_____

Unit 19
Kicking the Habit

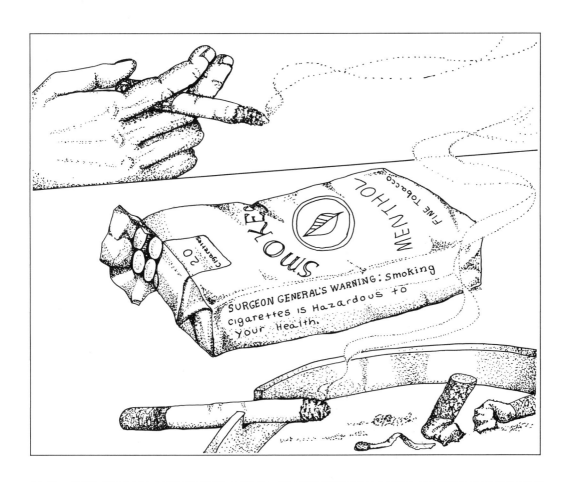

A. Vocabulary Preview

These words appear in Part C. Match each word with its definition. Match the following:

_____	1. picked up	a. until
		b. self-control, personal strength
_____	2. kick	c. started (a habit)
_____	3. irritable	d. attempts
_____	4. efforts	e. said with pride and egoism
_____	5. up to	f. get rid of, eliminate (a habit)
_____	6. will power	g. easily angered
_____	7. claimed	h. try to get someone to do something bad
_____	8. acknowledged	i. declared to be true
_____	9. boasted	j. admitted to be true
_____	10. tempt	

B. Reading Preview

Read the paragraph in Part C and answer these questions with *Yes* or *No*.

1. Has she picked up any bad habits? _____

2. Has she started eating too much? _____

3. Has she become relaxed and easygoing? _____

4. Has she avoided anyone? _____

5. Has she told her friends? _____

6. Has she started to smoke again? _____

C. Read the following:

Kicking the Habit

(1) I have not smoked a cigarette for three weeks. (2) During this time I have picked up some new habits. (3) For example, I have started eating between meals, chewing gum, and drinking sodas. (4) I have also had some unexpected problems. (5) I have become extremely nervous. (6) My friends have noticed my nervousness. (7) Occasionally, I have been irritable and impatient with them. (8) Fortunately, they have made sincere efforts to understand me during this difficult time. (9) I have avoided my friends who smoke. (10) I have not wanted them to tempt me to start smoking again. (11) Up to now, I have succeeded in not smoking. (12) This success has increased my will power to "kick the habit."

D. Write Away

1.   Marilyn has also stopped smoking. Write about her.

Your first sentence: **Marilyn has not smoked a cigarette for three weeks.**

2.   Write about Marilyn's efforts to stop smoking last week.

Your first sentence: **Marilyn did not smoke a cigarette last week.**

NOTE: Change **this** to **that** in (2), (8), and (12). In (11), change **Up to now** to **Up to then.**

3. When you saw Marilyn last weekend, she told you about her efforts to stop smoking. Write about what she told you.

Your first sentence: **Marilyn had not smoked a cigarette for two weeks when I saw her last week.**

NOTE: Change **this** to **that** in (2), (8), and (12). In (8), omit **have**. In (9), change **now** to **then**.

4. Report what Marilyn said.

In (1), use **She said that . . . .**

Your first sentence: **She said that she had not smoked a cigarette for three weeks.**

In (2), use **She complained that . . . .**
In (3), use **For example, she admitted that . . . .**
In (4), use **She commented that . . . .**
In (5), use **She claimed that . . . .**
In (6), use **She added that . . . .**
In (7), use **She acknowledged that . . . .**
In (8), use **She stated that . . . .**
In (9), use **She announced that . . . .**
In (10), use **She explained that . . . .**
In (11), use **She boasted that . . . .**
In (12), use **She insisted that . . . .**

5. Rewrite the paragraph, omitting the numbers. Follow the directions below:

Combine (1) and (2) with **, but.**
Do not change (3) and (4).
Combine (5) and (6) with **, and.**

Combine (7) and (8) with **, but.**
Combine (9) and (10) with **because.**
Combine (11) and (12) with **, and.**

E.   Writing Follow-Up

Everybody probably has at least one bad habit. What is yours? What have you done to stop it? Write a paragraph about it.

My Worst Habit

_____

_____

_____

_____

_____

_____

_____

Unit 20

Prevent
a Burglary

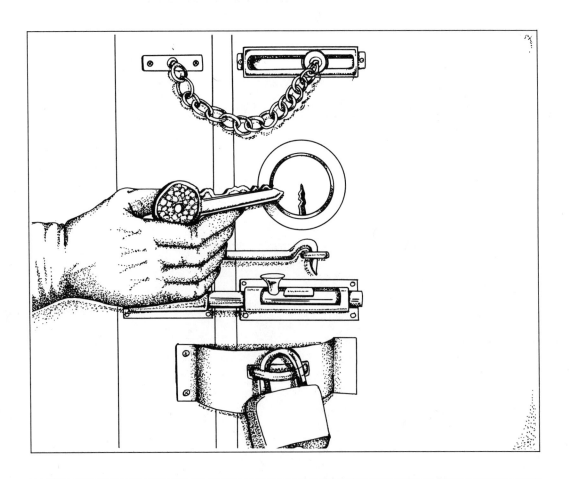

A.   Vocabulary Preview

These words appear in Part C. Match each word with its definition.

_____ 1. widow

_____ 2. urge

_____ 3. trustworthy

_____ 4. destination

_____ 5. install

_____ 6. delivery

a. the act of taking something to somebody

b. dependable

c. recommend strongly, try to convince

d. to set up something ready for use

e. woman whose husband has died

f. place where someone is going

B.   Reading Preview

Read the paragraph in Part C and connect the following:

a. Leave a key with
b. Install locks
c. Close securely
d. Leave on
e. Arrange for
f. Stop
g. Ask a neighbor
h. Notify
i. Tell a friend

all the windows
a dependable friend
a light
someone to pick up the
   mail
on the doors
the police about your trip
where you will be
to watch your place
the delivery of the
   newspaper

C. Read the following:

Prevent a Burglary

All over the world, burglaries are increasing. When people go on vacation, they worry about leaving their homes. Here is a list of questions to help prevent a burglary when you go away.

(1)   Have you installed strong locks on the doors?
(2)   Have you locked them?
(3)   Have you closed all the windows securely?
(4)   Have you left a light on?
(5)   Have you arranged for someone to pick up your mail?
(6)   Have you stopped the newspaper delivery?
(7)   Have you asked a neighbor to watch the house or apartment?
(8)   Have you notified the police about your trip?
(9)   Have you left a key with a trustworthy friend?
(10) Have you given him or her the address of your destination?

D. Write Away

1.   Pretend that you were away. When you return home, you discover that a burglar has been in your house. When the police arrive, they ask these questions. Write their questions.

Your first sentence: **Did you install strong locks on the doors?**

2.   Report to a friend what the police asked you.

Your first sentence: **The police asked me if/whether I had installed strong locks on the doors.**

3.   Now prepare a report for the police. Tell what you did by combining sentences (1) and (2), (3) and (4), (5) and (6), (7) and (8), and (9) and (10) in the following way.

Your first sentence: **After installing strong locks on the doors, I locked them.**

4.   Write the things that you remembered to do.

Your first sentence: **I remembered to install strong locks on the doors.**

5.   Write the things that a friend suggested that you do.

Your first sentence: **A friend suggested that I install strong locks on the doors.**

6.   Write the things you would suggest to a widow who lives alone.

In (1), use **would suggest**.

Your first sentence: **I would suggest that she install strong locks on the doors.**

In (2), use **would recommend**.
In (3), use **would urge**.
In (4), use **would advise**.
In (5), use **would propose**.
In (6), use **would suggest**.
In (7), use **would demand**.
In (8), use **would ask**.
In (9), use **would insist**.
In (10), use **would request**.

7.   Write a report for the insurance company about what you did. Omit the numbers.

Combine (1) and (2); use **First,** before (1).

Your first sentence: **First, I installed strong locks on the doors and locked them.**

Combine (3) and (4); use **Then,** before (3).
Combine (5) and (6); use **Next,** before (5).
Combine (7) and (8); use **After that,** before (7).
Combine (9) and (10); use **Finally,** before (9).

E.   Writing Follow-Up

Write a paragraph and tell what you did to make your household secure while you were away.

_____

_____

_____

_____

_____

_____

_____

_____

Unit 21

A High-Level Job

A. Vocabulary Preview

Complete these sentences. Use these words: *urge
skycraper   sharp   convince   wax   break*

1. A _____ is a very tall building.

2. "He arrived exactly at 5" is another way of saying "He
    arrived at five o'clock _____."

3. A _____ is a short period of time away from
    one's work for coffee or rest.

4. When you recommend strongly that a person do some-
    thing, you _____ him or her to do it.

5. If you want to make a floor appear smooth and shiny,
    you have to _____ it.

6. If you want to make someone feel certain about your
    point of view, you must persuade or _____ that
    person.

B. Reading Preview

Read the paragraph in Part C and connect the following:

a. wax   the view
b. wash   work
c. report to   time cards
d. supervise   floors

e. sign   desks and cabinets
f. dust   carpets
g. vacuum   workers
h. take   windows
i. enjoy   a break

C.   Read the following:

A High-Level Job

(1) Jacob Anders has a high-level job. (2) He supervises workers who clean skyscrapers at night. (3) He makes the cleaning staff report to work at 5:30 P.M. sharp. (4) He has them sign their time cards. (5) Then, he has them pick up their work assignments. (6) He helps them prepare their cleaning equipment. (7) Jacob makes them dust the desks and filing cabinets. (8) He has them vacuum the carpets and empty the ash trays and wastebaskets. (9) Once a month, he makes them wax the floors and wash the windows. (10) In spite of the hard work, Jacob helps his cleaning staff feel enthusiastic about their jobs. (11) He lets them take short breaks. (12) He lets them work alone if they wish. (13) Or, if they prefer, he lets them work in pairs. (14) Occasionally, after a lonely night's work, Jacob lets the workers enjoy the view from the 110th floor.

D.   Write Away

1.   Jacob retired last year. Write about his past.

Your first sentence: **Last year Jacob Anders had a high-level job.**

2.   Rewrite the model paragraph, substituting the following main verbs. Do not change anything in (1) and (2).

In (3), use **require**.

Your third sentence: **He requires the cleaning staff to report to work at 5:30 P.M. sharp.**

In (4), use **remind**.
In (5), use **ask**.
In (6), use **tell**.
In (7), use **order**.
In (8), use **urge**.
In (9), use **advise**.
In (10), use **encourage**.
In (11), use **convince**.
In (12), use **permit**.
In (13), use **allow**.
In (14), use **invite**.

3.   Using the verbs you used in exercise 2, rewrite the paragraph in the *past* tense. In (1) and (2), use *used to*. Omit the numbers.

Your first three sentences:

1. **Jacob Anders used to have a high-level job.**
2. **He used to supervise workers who cleaned skyscrapers at night.**
3. **He required them to report to work at 5:30 P.M. sharp.**

D.   Writing Follow-Up

Imagine you are writing a job description. Write about what your supervisor has you do. Mention five things at least.

Job Description

_____

_____

_____

_____

_____

_____

_____

Unit 22

The Big Light

A.   Vocabulary Preview

These words appear in Part C. Match each word with its definition.

_____ 1. to set

_____ 2. to splash

_____ 3. to flash

_____ 4. foggy

_____ 5. to cut through

_____ 6. huge

a. to reach across to another point or destination
b. to break (as water does) on rocks or the shore
c. to make a light turn on and off
d. very large
e. unclear and cloudy
f. to go down in the west (as the sun does)

B.   Reading Preview

Read the paragraph in Part C. Then connect the following:

a. orange	room
b. calm	night
c. huge	island
d. lonely	sea
e. rocky	job
f. tall	light
g. round	sky
h. foggy	scene
i. rare	tower

C. Read the following:

1. a. The sea is calm.
    b. It is peaceful.
    c. The sun is setting.
    d. It is setting in the sky.
    e. The sky is orange.

2. a. This sunset is a signal for Lucy.
    b. Lucy begins her job.
    c. Her job is lonely.

3. a. She is a lighthouse keeper.
    b. This lighthouse keeper is on an island.
    c. The island is rocky.
    d. She is one of the few people.
    e. These people climb the long stairs.
    f. Their climb is regular.
    g. The stairs go up to the giant light.

4. a. Lucy's lighthouse is a tower.
    b. The tower is tall.
    c. It is white.
    d. On top there is a room.
    e. It is round.

5. a. Inside this room the light sits.
    b. The light is powerful.

6. a. It is dark now.
    b. The darkness is complete.
    c. Lucy hears the waves.
    d. The waves are splashing on the rocks.
    e. The rocks are below the lighthouse.

7. a.   Up above, the light begins to flash.
    b.   The light is huge.
    c.   Its flash is regular.

8. a.   The light cuts through the night.
    b.   The night is foggy.
    c.   The light cuts through to a ship.
    d.   The ship is passing.
    e.   It is passing near the island.

9. a.   The ship answers.
    b.   The answer is: "All is well here."

10. a.   This scene is rare these days.
    b.   Lighthouses are becoming computerized.
    c.   Lighthouse keepers like Lucy are leaving their jobs.
    d.   Their jobs are lonely.
    e.   Their jobs are far away from the human crowds.

NOTE: Use **as** before 10b.

D.   Write Away

Combine the sentences in Part C. Write each group as one sentence.

E.   Writing Follow-Up

Describe a beautiful or peaceful place in your country. Answer these questions:

What is it?
Where is it?
Who lives there?
Why is it beautiful or peaceful?

_____

_____

_____

_____

_____

_____

_____

_____

Unit 23

A Friend
to All

A. Vocabulary Preview

These words appear in Part C. Match each word with its definition.

_____ 1. founded

_____ 2. humanitarian

_____ 3. pacifists

_____ 4. defensive

_____ 5. sacred

_____ 6. overcome

_____ 7. quake and tremble

_____ 8. scorn

_____ 9. badge of honor

_____ 10. significant

a. holy, with great religious respect
b. important
c. disrespect, hatred
d. shake
e. sign of respect
f. helping other people
g. started
h. protective of oneself against violence
i. believers in nonviolence
j. defeat, fight successfully to defeat

B. Reading Preview

Read the sentences in Part C. Then decide whether these statements are *True (T)* or *False (F)*. Circle the correct letter.

T   F   1. The Quakers are no longer a religious group.

T   F   2. The number of Quakers is surprisingly small.

T   F   3. The Quakers believe in self-defense.

T   F   4. The Quakers did not take sides in the Vietnam War.

T   F   5. The Quakers try to solve all human problems without violence.

T   F   6. Since their beginning, the Quakers have been highly respected.

C. Read the following:

1. a. The Religious Society of Friends is a religious group.
    b. It is special.
    c. Its members are called Quakers.

2. a. George Fox founded this society.
    b. He was an Englishman.
    c. He did this in 1647.

3. a. Three hundred years later, this organization won the Nobel Peace Prize.
    b. It won the prize for its work.
    c. Its work was humanitarian.

4. a. The Quakers are pacifists.
    b. They refuse to fight in all wars.
    c. They do this even in defensive wars.

5. a. Their pacifism comes from three beliefs.
    b. They believe that each human life is sacred.
    c. They believe that each person is a child of God.
    d. They believe that love can overcome hatred.
    e. They believe that love can overcome prejudice.
    f. They believe that love can overcome fear.

6. a. The Quakers seek solutions to human problems.
   b. The solutions are nonviolent.
   c. These problems may exist between Catholics and Protestants.
   d. These problems may exist between Jews and Arabs.
   e. These problems may exist between communists and capitalists.
   f. These problems may exist between races.

7. a. The Vietnam War is a good example.
   b. The war ended in 1974.
   c. It is an example of how the Quakers work.

8. a. In this war the Quakers helped both sides.
   b. They did this by giving them medical supplies.
   c. They did this by giving them farming equipment.
   d. They did this by giving them industrial materials.

9. a. In the seventeenth century, members of this sect had a belief.
   b. The sect was religious.
   c. This belief was unusual.

10. a. They believed that true believers had to quake.
    b. They believed that true believers had to tremble.
    c. They did these things when they prayed to God.

11. a. As a result, their enemies called them Quakers.
    b. For centuries, the word Quaker was used.
    c. It was used with scorn.
    d. Now it is a badge of honor.

12. a. The Religious Society of Friends is not a powerful organization.
   b. It has only about 200,000 members worldwide.
   c. The Quaker influence is great.
   d. Its members are very active.

13. a. For example, in the United States there are only 120,000 Quakers.
   b. They operate 64 children's schools.
   c. They operate 14 colleges.
   d. They are active in the movements of justice for American Indians.
   e. They are active in the movements of justice for prisoners.
   f. They are active in the movements of justice for migrant workers.
   h. They are active in the movements of justice for the poor.
   i. They are active in the movements of justice for the sick.

14. a. The Quakers' beliefs in peaceful, creative action have produced change.
   b. This change is significant.
   c. This change is social.
   d. This change is throughout the world.

D. Write Away

Combine the sentences in Part C. Write each group as one sentence.

E.   Writing Follow-Up

Write about a special group in your country that tries to help people. Answer these questions:

Who started the organization?
How old is it?
How has it helped people?
What do people think of this organization?

_____

_____

_____

_____

_____

_____

_____

_____

Unit 24

The Hope Diamond

A. Vocabulary Preview

These words appear in Part C. Match each word with its definition.

_____   1. get engaged

_____   2. a curse

_____   3. idol

_____   4. tragic

_____   5. carats

_____   6. crown jewels

_____   7. associated

_____   8. under suspicious circumstances

_____   9. guillotine

_____ 10. insane

_____ 11. exorcism

_____ 12. superstitious

a. crazy
b. a way of executing, killing a prisoner
c. a cause of bad luck
d. believing in bad or good luck
e. valuables belonging to a king and queen
f. very sad
g. announce plans to get married
h. a religious ceremony to drive away evil
i. statue that people worship in ceremonies
j. connected in one's mind
k. unsure, uncertain ways
l. measures of weight to show the size of a diamond

B.   Reading Preview

Read the sentences in Part C. Then decide whether these statements are *True (T)* or *False (F)*. Circle the correct letter.

T   F   1. The Hope Diamond is owned by a jeweler today.

T   F   2. The diamond first belonged to a king.

T   F   3. The diamond came from Asia.

T   F   4. Most people who owned the diamond had bad luck.

T   F   5. The Hope Diamond really has a curse.

T   F   6. The diamond is now in Europe.

T   F   7. The diamond has been on at least three continents.

T   F   8. The jeweler gave the diamond to a museum because he was afraid of its curse.

C.   Read the following:

1. a.   Most people are interested in diamonds.
    b.   They are valuable stones.

2. a.   In the United States, most women receive a diamond ring.
    b.   They do this when they get engaged.

3. a. One diamond is famous.
   b. Its fame is particular.
   c. It has brought bad luck to some of its owners.

4. a. This is the Hope Diamond.
   b. The Hope Diamond is valuable.
   c. Its value is extreme.

5. a. Some still say that the Hope Diamond has a curse.
   b. The curse began when a thief stole it.
   c. He stole it from an idol.
   d. The idol was Hindu.
   e. It was in India.
   f. People value it for its perfect quality.
   g. They value it for its deep blue color.

6. a. The Hope Diamond is not a ring.
   b. It is too large.

7. a. For that reason, it hangs on a chain.
   b. The chain is like a necklace.

8. a. People are fascinated by the Hope Diamond.
   b. It has a history.
   c. Its history is vivid.
   d. Its history is tragic.

9. a. In the seventeenth century a Frenchman brought a diamond to France.
   b. It had 112 carats.
   c. He brought it from India.

10. a. In 1668 the Frenchman sold the diamond.
    b. He sold it to King Louis XIV.
    c. It became a part of the French crown jewels.

11. a.   After the French revolution a diamond ap-
          peared in London.
    b.   It was probably the same one.
    c.   In London, Thomas Hope bought it.
    d.   Thomas Hope was a wealthy banker.

NOTE: Begin new paragraph.

12. a.   Many people suffered bad luck.
    b.   They were associated with the diamond.

13. a.   The Frenchman died.
    b.   He first brought the diamond from India.
    c.   His death was under suspicious circumstances.

14. a.   Marie Antoinette lost her head in the guillotine.
    b.   She was queen of France.
    c.   It was in 1793.

15. a.   Thomas Hope later lost all his money.
    b.   He was wealthy.
    c.   He was from London.
    d.   He was the banker.

16. a.   In 1912 a wealthy woman became the owner of
          the stone.
    b.   She was American.
    c.   Her life changed.
    d.   The change was tragic.

17. a.   Her two children died.
    b.   Their deaths were unexpected.
    c.   Her husband became an alcoholic.
    d.   He later went insane.

18. a.   She took the diamond to a priest.
     b.   The priest performed an exorcism.
     c.   He did this to get rid of the diamond's curse.
     d.   The curse was evil.

19. a.   Over the years the Hope Diamond changed hands many times.
     b.   This diamond is world famous.
     c.   A jeweler bought it.
     d.   He was from New York.

NOTE: Use **until** before 19c.

20. a.   He owned the diamond.
     b.   Some people refused to travel with him.
     c.   They feared the diamond's curse.
     d.   Its curse was tragic.

NOTE: Use **When** before 20a.

21. a.   The jeweler was not superstitious.
     b.   A few years ago he gave the diamond to a museum.
     c.   The museum is the Smithsonian Institute.
     d.   It is in Washington, D.C.

22. a.   Perhaps he believed the words of a song.
     b.   The song was popular.
     c.   It was from a musical.
     d.   The musical was American.
     e.   The song said that diamonds are a girl's best friend.

D.   Write Away

Combine the sentences above. Write each group as one sentence.

E.   Writing Follow-Up

On your own paper, write about the jewelry in your country. Answer these questions:

On what occasions do people give jewelry as gifts?
What kind of jewelry do they give?
Who wears it?
What does it mean?

Unit 25

A Little White Lie

A. Vocabulary Preview

These expressions appear in Part C. Match each expression with its definition.

_____ 1. something you
            harmlessly say
            that is not true

_____ 2. What's the
            matter?

_____ 3. Is she not well?

_____ 4. She's asleep now.

_____ 5. Her stomach
            hurts.

_____ 6. She has a
            temperature.

a. Is she sick?
b. She has a
   stomachache.
c. She's running a
   fever.
d. What's wrong?
e. A white lie
f. She's sleeping
   now.

B. Reading Preview

Before you read Part C, circle your answer. Check your answers _after_ you read the passage.

1. The caller is really a (teacher, boy, girl, mother).

2. The caller probably _is_ (sick, asleep, running a fever,

    not interested in school).

3. The caller speaks to (a teacher,   the principal,

    her mother,   another student).

4. At the end the teacher (speaks to the mother,

    is very understanding,   knows the truth,

    asks a lot of questions).

C. Read the following:

Caller: (1) Is this the Second Street School?
Teacher: (2) Yes, it is.
Caller: (3) Lillian Black isn't coming to school today.
Teacher: (4) Oh, is she sick?
Caller: (5) Yes, she is.   (6) She's sleeping now.
Teacher: (7) Oh, that's too bad.   (8) What's wrong with her?
Caller: (9) She's running a fever.   (10) She also has a stomachache.
Teacher: (11) That *is* bad. (pause)   (12) Who's speaking?
Caller: (13) (pause) It's my mother.

D. Write Away

1. You are the teacher. Report this conversation to your school principal, use words like:

She (I) asked (if) . . . . to report questions answered with *yes* or *no*.
She (I) said (that) . . . . to report statements.

Your first two sentences:

1. **She asked if this was the Second Street School.**
2. **I said that it was.**

NOTE: Omit the words **Yes** and **Oh**. In (8) and (12), do not use **if** after **asked**. In (13), change **my** to **her**.

2.   Combine the following sentences with **After**.

(1) and (3) with **After asking if . . . , she said that . . . .**

Your first sentence: **After asking if this was the Second Street School, she said that she wasn't coming to school today.**

(2) and (4) with **After saying that . . . , I asked if . . . .**
(5) and (6) with **After saying that . . . , she said that . . . .**
(7) and (8) with **After saying that . . . , I asked . . . .**
(9) and (10) with **After saying that . . . , she said that . . . .**
(11) and (12) with **After saying that . . . , I asked . . . .**
Complete (13) with this sentence **After saying that . . . ,
    she hung up the phone.**

3.   Rewrite the sentences from exercise 1 in one paragraph. Omit the numbers. Use the following information:

In (1), use **The caller asked if . . . .**
In (2), use **The teacher said that . . . .**
In (3), use **The caller said that Lillian Black . . . .**
In (4), (5) and (6), use **The teacher asked if . . . , and the
    caller answered that . . . , but . . . .**
In (7) and (8), use **Her teacher said that . . . and then
    asked . . . .**
In (9) and (10), use **The caller said that . . . and . . . .**
In (11) and (12), use **The teacher said that . . . and then
    asked . . . .**
In (13), use **The caller replied that . . . .**

D. Writing Follow-Up

Write a note to a teacher explaining that your child (or brother/sister) did not attend school one day. Be sure to include this information:

date of note
name of teacher
student's full name
date of absence
reason for absence
your name

_____

_____

_____

_____

_____

_____.

_____

Unit 26

The Champ

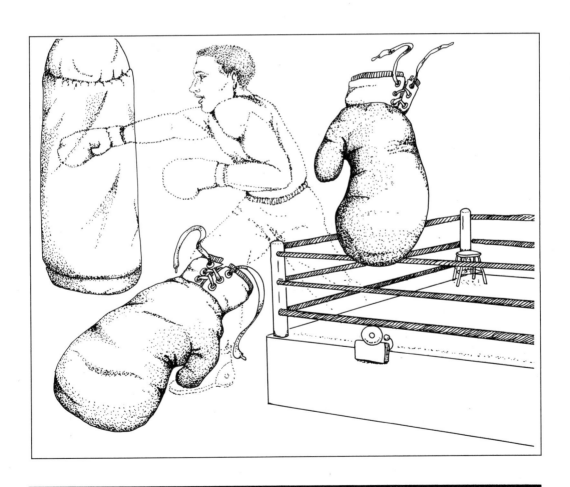

A. Vocabulary Preview

These words appear in Part C. Match each word with its definition.

_____ 1. reporter

_____ 2. opponent

_____ 3. manager

_____ 4. match

_____ 5. terribly proud

_____ 6. retiring

_____ 7. birthplace

a. where a person was born
b. a boxing competition
c. very honored/content
d. a person who supervises a boxer's training
e. journalist
f. stopping one's career
g. person who competes with another

B. Reading Preview

After you read Part C, answer *True (T)* or *False (F)*.

T   F   1. Woody is at the beginning of his boxing career.

T   F   2. Woody was born in Reno, Nevada.

T   F   3. Woody's next match is in three years.

T   F   4. Woody's going to retire at 35.

T   F   5. Woody's next opponent is Buzz Bonham.

T   F   6. Woody's manager is Sugar Ray Frontham.

C. Read the following:

Hank, a sports reporter, is planning to interview Woody
Brewster, a champion boxer. These are the *questions* that
Hank's boss has prepared.

   (1)   "What is Woody's full name?"
   (2)   "How old is Woody?"
   (3)   "Where is Woody's birthplace?"
   (4)   "Who is Woody's manager?"
   (5)   "Who is Woody's next opponent?"
   (6)   "When is Woody's next match?"
   (7)   "Where is Woody's next match?"
   (8)   "When is Woody planning to stop boxing?"
   (9)   "What is Woody going to do after retiring?"
(10)   "Why is Woody terribly proud?"

These are Woody's *answers*.

   (1)   "My full name is Woodrow Brewster."
   (2)   "I'm 32 years old."
   (3)   "My birthplace is Louisville, Kentucky."
   (4)   "My manager is Buzz Bonham."
   (5)   "My next opponent is Sugar Ray Frontham."
   (6)   "My next match is next month."
   (7)   "My next match is in Reno, Nevada."
   (8)   "I'm planning to stop boxing in three years."
   (9)   "I'm going to help young people."
(10)   "I'm proud because I'm the *Champ!*"

D. Write Away

1. You are at the press conference. Rewrite the questions, follow the example sentence below.

In (1), use **Hank wants to know . . . .**

Your first sentence: **Hank wants to know what Woody's full name is.**

In (2), use **Hank wants to find out . . . .**
In (3), use **Hank has to know . . . .**
In (4), use **Hank plans to ask . . . .**
In (5), use **Hank wonders . . . .**
In (6), use **Hank needs to know . . . .**
In (7), use **Hank asks . . . .**
In (8), use **Hank wants to know . . . .**
In (9), use **Hank has no idea . . . .**

2. Now repeat what Hank *wanted* to know. Rewrite the sentences you wrote in exercise 1.

Your first sentence: **Hank wanted to know what Woody's full name was.**

3. Hank is repeating Woody's *answers* to someone else. Write all his answers, imitating the first sentence below.

Your first sentence: **Woody says that his full name is Woodrow Brewster.**

4. Hank reported Woody's answers to his newspaper.

In (1), use **Woody stated that . . . .**

Your first sentence: **Woody stated that his full name was Woodrow Brewster.**

In (2), use **Woody said that . . . .**
In (3), use **Woody replied that . . . .**
In (4), use **Woody answered that . . . .**
In (5), use **Woody announced that . . . .**
In (6), use **Woody emphasized that . . . .**
In (7), use **Woody reported that . . . .**
In (8), use **Woody insisted that . . . .**
In (9), use **Woody boasted that . . . .**

E.   Writing Follow-Up

1.   If you had the opportunity to interview someone famous, what questions would you ask? Write five questions.

2.   What do you think the person's answers would be? Write them.

3.   Now rewrite the questions and answers in reported speech in a paragraph. Give your paragraph a title.

_____

_____

_____

_____

_____

_____

_____

_____

Unit 27

The Reluctant Boyfriend

A. Vocabulary Preview

These words relate to the wedding discussed in Part C. Circle the word or phrase that is different in each group. Explain why it is different.

1. bridal gown   tuxedo   ring

2. groom   maid of honor   bride

3. best man   bride   groom

4. reception   wedding   guest

5. to pay for   to cost   to get married

6. when   where   why

B. Reading Preview

Read the sentences in Part C. Then answer *True*, *False*, or *I don't know*.

1. _____ Julia wants to get married.

2. _____ Julia and George have many friends.

3. _____ Julia is very flexible.

4. _____ George wants to pay for the wedding.

5. _____ George and Julia seem to agree on the wedding plans.

C. Read the following:

(1) George: When are we getting married?
(2) Julia: Whenever you decide.
(3) George: Where are we having the wedding?
(4) Julia: Wherever you choose.
(5) George: Who's going to be the best man or the maid of honor?
(6) Julia: Who(m)ever you want.
(7) George: What are we serving at the reception?
(8) Julia: Whatever you like.
(9) George: Which friends are we going to ask to be in the wedding?
(10) Julia: The friends you want to ask.
(11) George: How many guests are we inviting?
(12) Julia: As many guests as you wish.
(13) George: How much will the rings cost?
(14) Julia: As much as you are willing to spend.
(15) George: Hey, why do I have to pay for everything?
(16) Julia: Because you are the one who wants to get married.

D. Write Away

1. Julia told her mother what George asked her. Write the questions that Julia reported to her mother.

Your first sentence: **George asked me when we were getting married.**

2.   George told his father about their conversation. Using the following sentence as a model, write down what George reported to his father.

Your first sentence: **Julia said that we were getting married whenever I decided.**

NOTE: In (5) and (6), use **the best man or the maid of honor** after **that**. In (7) and (8), put **at the reception** at the end of the sentence. In (8) and (9), put **in the wedding** at the end of the sentence.

3.   Some of Julia's answers in the dialogue are not complete. Below are the missing parts of her answers. Combine her answers with the parts below.

In (2), add . . . **is all right with me.**

Your first sentence: **Whenever you decide is all right with me.**

In (4), add . . . **is acceptable to me.**
In (6), add . . . **suits me.**
In (8), add . . . **will be delicious.**
In (10), add . . . **will be the guests.**
In (12), **We can invite . . . .**
In (14), **The wedding will cost . . . .**
In (16), add . . . , **you have to pay for the wedding.**

E. Writing Follow-Up

Describe a typical wedding in your country. Give details about the place, the members of the wedding, the celebration before or after the wedding, the guests, and the food. Who pays for the wedding?

_____

_____

_____

_____

_____

_____

_____

_____

Unit 28

Signs of
the Road

A.

B.

C.

D.

E.

F.

G.

H.

I.

J.

A. Vocabulary Preview

Match each sign on page 145 with its meaning.

_____   1. Dangerous Curve. Drive Carefully.

_____   2. No Entry

_____   3. No Parking

_____   4. Watch for Falling Rock

_____   5. No Passing

_____   6. Slippery Road. Drive Slowly.

_____   7. No Left Turn

_____   8. Watch for Children

_____   9. No Right Turn

_____   10. People Working. Drive Cautiously.

B. Reading Preview

Which sign(s) is/are:

_____   a. probably near a school?

_____   b. at the intersection of a one-way street?

_____   c. probably in the mountains?

_____   d. probably in a city?

_____   e. informative about road conditions?

_____   f. informative about what *not to do*?

_____   g. informative about what *to do*?

C. Write Away

1.   Look at the road signs and write what you *should* or *should not* do for each one.

Your first sentence: **You should not turn left.**

2.   Look at pictures A, B, C, D, E, and I. Write what you *can't do.*

Your first sentence: **You can't turn left.**

3.   Use the expressions below and write a complete sentence about pictures A, B, D, E, and I.

In (A), use **It's illegal to . . . .**

Your first sentence: **It's illegal to turn left.**

In (B), use **It's unsafe to . . . .**
In (D), use **It's unlawful to . . . .**
In (E), use **It's not legal to . . . .**
In (I), use **It's not safe to . . . .**

4.   Use the expressions below and write a complete sentence about pictures C, F, G, H, and J.

In (C), use **It's advisable to . . . .**
In (F), use **It's important to . . . .**
In (G), use **It's wise to . . . .**
In (H), use **It's best to . . . .**
In (J), use **It's necessary to . . . .**

5. Use the expressions below and write a complete sentence about pictures A, B, D, E, and I.

In (A), use . . . **is not permitted.**
In (B), use . . . **is not allowed.**
In (D), use . . . **is forbidden.**
In (E), use . . . **is prohibited.**
In (I), use . . . **is not permitted.**

6. Use the expressions below and write a complete sentence about pictures C, F, G, H, and J.

In (C), use **It's suggested that a driver . . . .**
In (F), use **It's recommended that a driver. . . .**
In (G), use **It's advised that a driver. . . .**
In (H), use **It's required that a driver. . . .**
In (J), use **It's suggested that a driver. . . .**

7. Describe the signs below and write what each sign means to a driver in one sentence.

Left Turn Only   Right Turn Only   Straight Ahead Only

Your first sentence: **This round sign with a white arrow pointing right means that a driver has to turn right.**

8.   Describe the signs below and write what each one means.

Telephone   Restaurant   Motel   Service
                                    Station

Your first sentence: **The sign with a picture of a telephone indicates that there is a telephone ahead.**

D.   Writing Follow-Up

Do you know of other public signs, such as those on trains
or in buildings? Describe the signs and write about their
meanings, or design your own sign. Describe it and write
about its meaning.

_____

_____

_____

_____

_____

_____

_____

_____

Unit 29

A Heartening Situation

Get plenty of exercise for a healthy heart.

A.   Vocabulary Preview

Circle the one word or phrase that is different in each
group. Explain.

1.   consume   drink   eliminate

2.   cut out smoking   cut down on smoking   stop

smoking

3.   butter   margarine   salt

4.   cheese   butter   milk

5.   relax   exercise   reach

6.   fat-free products   fatty food   whole-milk

products

B.   Reading Preview

Read the poster. Please put a check by those things that
are *good* for your health. Place an X by those that are *bad*
for your health.

_____ a. butter   _____ g. stress

_____ b. exercise   _____ h. fatty food

_____ c. margarine   _____ i. salt

_____ d. fat-free food   _____ j. smoking

_____ e. whole milk   _____ k. skimmed milk

_____ f. eggs   _____ l. dairy products

A Heartening Situation

Heart disease kills more people than any other illness. It is caused by high blood pressure, cholesterol in the blood, being overweight, or smoking. Until several years ago, Finland had the highest rate of heart disease in the world. As a result, public health officials in Finland released important information on how to cut down on heart disease. This poster shows the *DOs* and *DON'Ts*.

HEART DISEASE IS A KILLER!
DON'T LET IT KILL YOU.

DO
- (1) Cut out fatty foods!
- (2) Drink skimmed milk and use other fat-free dairy products.
- (3) Eliminate butter; use margarine instead.
- (4) Cut down on salt; use other seasonings instead.
- (5) Get plenty of exercise.
- (6) Learn how to control stress. Relax!

DON'T
- (1) Smoke!
- (2) Consume a lot of cheese and other dairy products.
- (3) Drink whole milk
- (4) Use butter
- (5) Eat so many eggs.
- (6) Reach for the salt shaker.

C. Write Away

1.   Write the things that the Finnish people *would have to do* in order to decrease heart disease. Use the list of *DOs* on the poster.

Your first sentence: **They would have to cut out fatty foods.**

2.   Write the things that the people would have to *stop doing* in order to decrease their heart disease. Use the list of *DON'Ts* on the poster.

In (1), use **stop.**

Your first sentence: **The people would have to stop smoking.**

In (2), use **cut down on.**
In (3), use **cease.**
In (4), use **cut out.**
In (5), use **refrain from.**
In (6), use **quit.**

3.   Write about the things that *would have happened unless* they did something. Use the *DOs* on the poster.

In (1), use . . . **might not lower the fat concentration in their blood.**

Your first sentence: **Unless they cut out fatty foods, they might not lower the fat concentration in their blood.**

In (2), use . . . **they could not decrease their consumption of fat.**

In (3), use . . . **the fat intake would probably not change.**

In (4), use . . . **their high blood pressure probably would persist.**

In (5), use . . . **they couldn't keep in good physical shape.**

In (6), use . . . **they would still suffer from hypertension.**

4.   Jaakki is from Finland. He has heart disease, and his doctor told him what to do about his illness. Write the doctor's instructions. Combine the phrases below with the *DOs* and *DON'Ts* on the poster.

DO

(a)   The doctor insisted that Jaakki . . . .
(b)   The doctor urged that he . . . .
(c)   The doctor suggested that he . . . .
(d)   The doctor requested that he . . . .
(e)   The doctor ordered that he . . . .
(f)   The doctor advised that he . . . .

DON'T

(g)   The doctor recommended that he . . . .
(h)   The doctor made the recommendation that he . . . .
(i)   The doctor made the suggestion that he . . . .
(j)   The doctor said it was necessary that he . . . .
(k)   The doctor said it was essential that he . . . .
(l)   The doctor said it was imperative that he . . . .

Your first sentence: **The doctor insisted that Jaakki cut out fatty foods.**

NOTE: For the *DON'Ts* (g) through (l): use **not** after **that he . . . .**

5.   Only five years later the Finnish people were proud of their progress. Heart attacks in men had decreased by 40%. Write about what *would have happened if they hadn't done something*. Use the *DON'T* information from the poster.

In (1), use **continued / heart disease (not) decrease.**

Your first sentence: **If they had continued smoking, their heart disease wouldn't have decreased.**

In (2), use **continued . . . their fat intake . . . become excessive.**
In (3), use **gone on . . . the fat levels in their blood . . . increased.**
In (4), use **persisted in . . . their health . . . not improved.**
In (5), use **continued . . . their cholesterol levels . . . remain high.**
In (6), use **kept on . . . their hypertension get worse.**

6.   Write the things *it had been necessary for the Finns to do*. Use the *DOs* and *DON'Ts* on the *poster*.

Your first sentence: **It had been necessary for the people to cut out fatty foods.**

D.   Writing Follow-Up

1.   Write a composition *on your own paper* by answering each question below in your own words. Give complete answers. Omit the numbers.

First paragraph: 1.   What illness causes the most deaths in the world?
2.   What are the four major causes of this illness?

Second paragraph: 1.   Until a few years ago, which country in the world had the highest death rate from heart disease?

2.   What did the people decide to do?

3.   What would they have to do about smoking?

4.   What would they have to do about dairy products?

5.   What would they have to do about salt, eggs, and fatty foods?

6.   What are some things they would have to start?

Third paragraph: 1.   Only five years later, how did the people feel about their progress? Why?

2.   What had happened?

2.   In every country some people have harmful eating and drinking habits. Write about them and what the people should do.

3.   There are harmful diseases in every country. Write about a harmful disease and discuss what people should do about it.

Unit 30

The Great Climb

A. Vocabulary Preview

These words appear in Part C. Match each word with its definition.

_____ 1. incident

_____ 2. caught sight

_____ 3. persuade

_____ 4. descend

_____ 5. platform

_____ 6. attempt

_____ 7. applaud

_____ 8. scene

a. change someone else's mind
b. try
c. go down
d. event
e. place to stand on
f. place or location
g. saw
h. clap one's hands

B. Reading Preview

Read the sentences in Part C. Then say if these statements are *True*, *False*, or *Unknown*.

1. _____ The climber was a professional.

2. _____ He finished his climb in the afternoon.

3. _____ The policemen persuaded the climber to get on the platform.

4. _____ The climber seemed very reasonable.

5. _____ The climber paid the fine.

6. _____ The mayor was trying to get re-elected.

C. Read the following:

1. a. Sometimes an incident can be dangerous.
    b. It can be adventurous at the same time.

2. a. For example, not long ago a toy designer climbed the World Trade Center.
    b. The World Trade Center has 110 stories.
    c. The World Trade Center is the tallest skyscraper in New York.

3. a. Pedestrians first caught sight of the man.
    b. It was in early morning.
    c. He was already half way up the building.

4. a. Soon the streets below filled with onlookers.
    b. They were excited.

5. a. Newspaper reporters rushed to the scene.
    b. Radio reporters rushed to the scene.
    c. TV reporters rushed to the scene.

6. a. The police also rushed to the scene in order to control the crowds.
    b. The police also rushed to the scene in order to direct the traffic.
    c. The police also rushed to the scene in order to persuade the climber to come down.

7. a. Afterwards, two policemen went to the top of the building.
   b. They descended to the level of the climber.
   c. They did this by using a special platform for washing windows.
   d. The platform was motorized.

8. a. Then the policemen asked the climber to stop climbing.
   b. The policemen asked the climber to return with them to the top of the building.

9. a. The climber refused to stop.
   b. He insisted on finishing the climb.
   c. By then, he was halfway up the building.

10. a. He pointed out that it was safer to finish the climb.
    b. It was safer to do that than to attempt to transfer to the platform.

11. a. The policemen understood the climber's reaction.
    b. They decided to accompany him up the building.
    c. They would do this until he reached the top.

12. a. On top of the building, the reporters applauded.
    b. On top of the building, the police applauded.
    c. They were waiting there.
    d. They did this when he stepped safely onto the roof.
    e. It was three and a half hours after he had begun.

13. a. He was a hero to most of the people after his
       climb.
    b. The police arrested him.
    c. They told him that he would have to pay
       $250,000 in damages.

NOTE: Before 13a, Use **Although**.

14. a. However, the next day the mayor held a news
       conference.
    b. They mayor was seeking re-election.
    c. The news conference was with the climber.
    d. The mayor reduced the fine to $1.10.
    e. That amounted to a penny for each floor the
       young man had climbed.

D. Write Away

Combine the sentences in Part C.

E. Writing Follow-Up

A few years ago another daredevil incident took place. Here are some of the details of the incident. Write a paragraph using these details. Use the title: "The Great Walk."

young circus acrobat
string a wire
between two buildings of the World Trade Center
for about half an hour
110 stories above the city streets
crowds
reporters
police . . . arrest
judge . . . court
*sentence: . . . free acrobatic performances for children
    in the park*

The Great Walk

_____

_____

_____

_____

_____

_____

_____

Unit 31

The Great Chase

A. Vocabulary Preview

These words appear in Part C. Match each word with its definition.

_____ 1.	blink	a. wonder or disbelief
_____ 2.	astonishment	b. open and shut (one's eyes)
_____ 3.	double-decker	c. having two floors/ levels
_____ 4.	step on the gas	d. chase or go after
		e. drivers (of cars)
_____ 5.	emerge	f. walkers on a street
_____ 6.	pedestrians	g. come out of or appear
_____ 7.	motorists	h. speed up
_____ 8.	pursue	i. driving slowly
_____ 9.	board	j. get on (a bus)
_____ 10.	cruising	

B. Reading Preview

Read the sentences in Part C. Then put these sentences into the correct time sequence. For the first sentence in the story, write 1 in the blank to the left.

_____ a. The police officers started to chase the bus, which headed for the park.

_____ b. Not long ago two young boys stole a large bus and started driving it through the crowded city streets.

_____ c. The police officers arrested the two young boys and took them away.

_____ d. Two police officers saw the bus and its young occupants and ordered them to stop.

_____ e. Seeing the garbage truck, the young driver stopped the bus.

_____ f. The boys ignored the officers' orders and speeded up.

_____ g. While chasing the bus through the park, the officers called for help, and soon other police cars, with lights flashing and sirens blowing, joined in the bus chase.

_____ h. On the parkway, a police officer stopped a large sanitation truck and told the driver to block the road in front of the bus.

C. Read the following:

1. a. A police officer's life is filled with events.
    b. These events are unexpected.
    c. Most of these events are tragic.
    d. Some of these events are funny.

2. a. Here is a story.
    b. It is amusing.
    c. My brother told it to me.
    d. My brother is a policeman.

3. a. He was cruising in a police car.
   b. His partner was cruising in a police car.
   c. Suddenly they saw something.
   d. It made them blink their eyes in disbelief.

NOTE: Use **when** before 3c.

4. a. A young boy was driving a bus up the street.
   b. It was a double-decker.
   c. Another kid was sitting behind him.

5. a. My brother leaned out of the car window.
   b. He ordered the young driver to stop.
   c. The boy stepped on the gas.
   d. The boy kept on going.

6. a. My brother began to chase the bus up the street.
   b. His partner began to chase the bus up the street.
   c. They continued across Central Park.
   d. They were headed toward the parkway.

7. a. The bus was screeching wildly around curves.
   b. It was traveling at 50 miles an hour.
   c. It emerged from the park.
   d. The police car was still behind it.

NOTE: Use **with** before 7d.

8. a. Pedestrians had to run to safety.
   b. Motorists had to pull over.
   c. They did this to avoid an accident.

9. a.   My brother was afraid to pursue the bus too fast.

     b.   His partner was afraid to pursue the bus too fast.

     c.   They didn't want to cause an accident.

10. a.   Meanwhile, they asked for help.

     b.   They did this over the police radio.

     c.   About 15 other police cars joined the chase.

     d.   Their red lights were flashing.

     e.   Their sirens were blowing loudly.

11. a.   The bus entered the parkway.

     b.   My brother saw a truck.

     c.   It was large.

     d.   It was used for garbage.

NOTE: Use **At the moment** before 11a.

12. a.   He stopped the truck.

     b.   He asked the driver to do something.

     c.   He said, "Drive quickly to 177th Street!"

     d.   They drove onto the parkway.

     e.   They blocked the traffic.

NOTE: Use **, where** after 12c.

13. a.   The bus came to a stop.

     b.   The two policemen boarded the bus.

     c.   They did this quickly.

     d.   They arrested the two boys.

     e.   They said they were 14 years old.

NOTE: Use **After** before 13a.

14. a.   My brother scratched his head.
    b.   He was astonished.

NOTE: Use **in** before 14b.

15. a.   The young driver did not hit anyone.
    b.   He did not hit anything.
    c.   He had driven the bus.
    d.   He had never before handled anything larger than a bicycle.
    e.   He had done this like a professional driver.

NOTE: Use **Without** before 15a.

D. Write Away

These are activities that were going on in the park during the bus chase. Change the second sentence of the following pairs into a modifying phrase with *-ing*. In sentences 1 and 3, use the *-ing* phrase at the end of the sentence.

EXAMPLE:
   1.   The young boy handled it like a pro.
   2.   He was driving a big double-decker bus through the park.

Your first sentence: **The young boy driving a big double-decker bus through the park handled it like a pro.**

1. a.   A young couple were walking through the park.
    b.   They were holding hands.

2. a.   A few people pushed and shoved to get out of the way of the bus.
    b.   They were running for safety.

3. a. A dog started to chase the bus.
   b. He was barking at all the activity.

4. a. A group of college students paid no attention to the commotion.
   b. They were smoking under a tree.

5. a. Two old ladies stopped talking and stared in amazement.
   b. They were sitting on a bench and talking to each other.

6. a. Some cyclists rode into the lake.
   b. They were fleeing from the bus.

7. a. Children pointed at the bus and laughed.
   b. They were playing on the grass.

8. a. Some people thought the whole thing was a scene from a movie.
   b. They were standing nearby.

E. Writing Follow-Up

Think of an incident (an accident, a fire, a crime, an adventure of some type) and write about it. *On your own paper,* tell the story from the beginning, including all the details in the order that they happened. Use these words if you can: *First, Next, Then, After that, Afterwards, Finally,*

Unit 32

It All Started with Zeus

A. Vocabulary Preview

These words appear in Part C. Match each word with its definition.

_____ 1. dedicated to

_____ 2. conquest

_____ 3. worship

_____ 4. forbidden

_____ 5. influential

_____ 6. sponsor

_____ 7. influence (verb)

_____ 8. authorities

a. persons in powerful positions
b. having power/respect over other people
c. not allowed
d. have an effect on
e. in honor of
f. victory in war
g. show religious respect
h. be officially responsible for (an event)

B. Reading Preview

Read the sentences in Part C. Then say if these statements are *True, False,* or *Unknown.*

_____ 1. The first Olympic Games were held over 2000 years ago.

_____ 2. Women participated in the first games.

_____ 3. Each original athlete in the first games represented a different country.

_____ 4. The Romans sponsored the later Olympics.

_____ 5. The modern Olympic Games started
again in the twentieth century.

_____ 6. Foreigners do not compete in the modern
games.

C. Read the following:

1. a.   The first Olympic Games were probably held in
776 B.C.
    b.   They were held by the Greeks.

2. a.   The games were dedicated to Zeus.
    b.   They were dedicated by the athletes.

3. a.   Zeus was worshiped at Olympia.
    b.   He was the most powerful Greek god.
    c.   The first games were held there.
    d.   The games were held by the Greek leaders.

NOTE: Use **where** before 3c; omit **there** in 3c.

4. a.   After the games the winners were welcomed as
heroes.
    b.   They were welcomed by their cities.

5. a.   In the first games, women were not allowed to
participate.
    b.   In the first games, foreigners were not allowed
to participate.
    c.   In the first games, slaves were not allowed to
participate.
    d.   They were not allowed by the officials.

6. a.   Women were also forbidden to watch the games.
    b.   They were forbidden by the authorities.

7. a. However, in the sixth century B.C., Olympic Games for women were organized.
   b. They were organized by Greek women.
   c. The women were influential.

8. a. After the Roman conquest of the Greek Empire, the games were stopped.
   b. They were stopped by the Roman leaders.

9. a. Then, in 1896, the first modern Olympic Games were organized.
   b. They were organized by a French nobleman.
   c. They were held in Athens.

10. a. Except during World War II, the Olympic Games have been sponsored every four years.
    b. They have been sponsored by an international committee.

11. a. In the ancient games, political differences were not noticed.
    b. They were not noticed by athletes.

12. a. However, the modern games are sometimes greatly influenced.
    b. They are influenced by political differences.

D. Write Away

Combine the sentences in Part C.

1.   After you combine the sentences, rewrite the paragraphs and tell *who did what.*

Your first sentence: **The Greeks held the first Olympic Games in 776 B.C.**

2.   Rewrite the paragraphs by telling only *what was done*. Omit the numbers. Do not change (12).

Your first sentence: **The first Olympic Games were held in 776 B.C.**

E.   Writing Follow-Up

Write about an important historical or sports event. Be sure to explain:

what it is
where it was started
when it was started
by whom it was started
why it was started

_____

_____

_____

_____

_____

_____

_____

Unit 33

The Engagement Party

You are invited to an engagement party

for

Sissy Cole and Fred Parkins

on

Friday, September 26, 1989

8 p.m.

47 Oxford Street

R.S.V.P. LaVerne Sunsteen

496-3811

A. Vocabulary Preview

These words appear in Part C. In the right column, find the word that is related to the first two words in each group. Then write the letter of that word in the blank next to the correct group.

_____ 1. engaged   married   a. sad

_____ 2. guests   friends   b. mailed

_____ 3. bitter   heartbroken   c. actress

_____ 4. prepared   wrote   d. neighbors

_____ 5. nurse   manager   e. accused

_____ 6. arrested   bigamy   f. single

B. Reading Preview

Read the following letter and then circle the correct answer.

1. (The neighbors, Her fiance, The police) gave the engagement party.

2. The party was for (Ida, Anna, Sissy).

3. Fred Parkins was _not_ (married, single, engaged).

4. (Bob, LaVerne, Mike) used to live in the same building.

5. Sissy called (the police, off the wedding, Bob).

6. Sissy was _not_ (happy, bitter, heartbroken) after the party.

C. Read the following:

The Engagement Party

January 20, 19——

Dear Bob:

How're you? We're all fine but very busy. I wish you'd been here last week. We had a really unusual party in my apartment. You know most of the people who came because they are old neighbors of yours in the building. Well, let me tell you some of the details.

(1) The neighbors gave an engagement party for Sissy, the only single girl in our building now.   (2) Ida, the registered nurse, prepared the guest list.   (3) Anna, the retired actress, wrote the invitations.   (4) Reuben, her grandson, mailed them for her.   (5) Mr. Faircloth, the English tailor, brought the food. (6) Mrs. Lipscombe, the landlady, prepared the drinks. (7) Mike, the building manager, decorated the apartment. (8) The guests, all neighbors and friends, brought gifts.

(9) All was going well until the police arrested Fred Parkins, Sissy's fiance.   (10) According to the police, two other women, still married to him, accused him of bigamy.   (11) The next day, Sissy, heartbroken and bitter, called off the wedding. It was a sad end to what should have been a happy event.

Sorry I don't have more time to write now. I'll telephone next week. Hope all's well with you.

Your friend,

La Verne

P.S. Sissy asked me for your address today. You'll probably hear from her soon.

D.   Write Away

1.   Below is a list of people who planned the party for
Sissy Cole:

Ida Fine prepared the guest list
Anna Shipper wrote the invitations
Reuben Shipper mailed the invitations
Harry Faircloth bought the food
Shirley Lipscombe prepared the drinks
Mike Yama decorated the apartment

Now write a report of this party for the neighborhood
newspaper. Use only the information in the list above and
rewrite the 11 sentences in paragraphs 2 and 3 in the letter. Write *what was done.*

Your first sentence: **Last week an engagement party
was given for Sissy Cole.**

2.   Rewrite the 11 sentences in paragraphs 2 and 3 by inserting **who is (are)** in each sentence.

Your first sentence: **Last week neighbors gave an engagement party for Sissy Cole, who is the only single
girl in our building.**

NOTE: In (8), (9), and (11), use **was** or **were**.

3.   Rewrite the sentences in exercise 2 like the sentences below.

Your first sentence: **Last week an engagement party was given for Sissy Cole, who is the only single girl in our building.**

4.   LaVerne wants to write this information in a letter to another friend, Bess, who does not know any of these people. Write the letter for LaVerne, making all the necessary changes. Try to vary your sentences using the techniques in exercises 1 and 2 above. Omit the numbers.

Begin with the following paragraph:

January 20, 19——

Dear Bess:

   Let me tell you about a really unusual party that we had last week in my apartment. You don't know any of these people, but here are the details.

Use the complete names of the people (see 1).
Change *the* to *a(n)* when necessary.
Combine (3) and (4) with **, and.**
Combine (5) and (6) with **, while.**
Omit the **P.S.**

E.   Writing Follow-Up

Write a newspaper article on a social event (a wedding, a meeting, a party) and give all the details, such as:

what the occasion was
when and where it was held
who was invited
who planned it
how it ended

_____

_____

_____

_____

_____

_____

_____

_____

Unit 34

Space Power

A.   Vocabulary Preview

These words appear in Part C. Match each word with its definition.

_____   1. permanent
_____   2. provide
_____   3. inhabitants
_____   4. huge
_____   5. convert
_____   6. abundant
_____   7. colonies
_____   8. microwaves

a. large or gigantic
b. change
c. plenty of or sufficient
d. occupants or residents
e. settlements in remote
   areas
f. make available
g. electric signals
h. lasting a long time

B.   Reading Preview

Read the paragraph in Part C. Then say if these statments are *True, False,* or *Unknown.*

_____ 1. Only government agencies will establish colonies in space.

_____ 2. Families will be sent to the space colonies.

_____ 3. The purpose of the plants is to change sunlight into electric power.

_____ 4. The electrical energy will be plentiful and clean.

_____ 5. The "new frontier" means space.

_____ 6. The space workers will not need to return to Earth.

C.   Read the following:

Space Power

(1) Within 25 years a number of national agencies and industrial corporations will establish permanent colonies in space.   (2) These groups will train the men and women who will live and work in the colonies.   (3) They will also provide food stores, shops, restaurants, gardens, hospitals, theaters, and schools for the inhabitants.   (4) Thousands of men and women will build and operate huge power plants.   (5) These plants will change sunlight into microwaves of energy.   (6) Then, large metal mirrors will send the microwaves to Earth.   (7) On Earth, gigantic energy plants will convert the microwaves into ordinary electricity.   (8) Thus, these space plants will produce an abundant and clean source of energy for people on Earth.   (9) In the near future, postal workers will deliver letters from relatives and friends from the new frontier.   (10) Maybe you will write such letters from space someday.

D.   Write Away

1.   Rewrite the passage to answer questions like *What will be established in space?*

Your first sentence: **Within 25 years permanent colonies in space will be established by a number of national agencies and industrial corporations.**

2.   Rewrite the passage and insert this additional information.

In (1) **decide to**

Your first sentence: **Within 25 years a number of national agencies and industrial corporations will decide to establish permanent colonies in space.**

In (2) **set up programs to**
In (3) **need to**
In (4) **will be recruited to**
In (5) **be used to**
In (6) **be assembled to**
In (7) **be utilized to**
In (8) **be able to**
In (9) **not find it unusual to**
In (10) **be in a place to**

3.   Rewrite the passage and insert this additional information.

In (1) **merge for the purpose of**

Your first sentence: **Within 25 years a number of national agencies and industrial corporations will merge for the purpose of establishing permanent colonies in space.**

In (2) **set up programs for**
In (3) **be responsible for**
In (4) **be paid for**
In (5) **be built for the purpose of**
In (6) **be capable of**
In (7) **have no difficulty in**

In (8) **be devoted to**
In (9) **make their living by**
In (10) **be involved in**

E.   Writing Follow-Up

What do the next 25 years look like for your country?
Write about a future project. Explain:

what it is
who will do it
where it will be done
why it will be done

_____

_____

_____

_____

_____

_____

_____

_____

Unit 35
Trends

A.   Vocabulary Preview

These words appear in Part C. Match each word with its definition.

_____ 1. vandalism

_____ 2. reject

_____ 3. status

_____ 4. values

_____ 5. priorities

_____ 6. conventional

_____ 7. investigate

_____ 8. alternative

_____ 9. oppose

_____ 10. ignore

a. following accepted customs
b. a choice for something different
c. refuse to notice
d. destruction of property
e. refuse to accept
f. be or act against
g. rank or class in society
h. things arranged in order of importance
i. people's ideas about the worth of certain things or ideas
j. examine carefully

B.   Reading Preview

Read the paragraph in Part C. Then place a check if you think the trend is positive and an X if you think it is negative. Discuss your answers.

_____ a. "I'm not drinking so much coffee."

_____ b. "Clothes don't really matter so much to me. I wear jeans most of the time."

_____ c. "Why should I go to college? I just want to be a carpenter."

_____ d. "Sure. I'd marry a person who isn't a member of my religion."

_____ e. "Let's get even with that woman! Break her car window."

_____ f. "Smoking makes me look more sophisticated."

_____ g. "I don't buy that company's products because it pollutes the environment."

_____ h. "Why can't I live alone? I don't have to get married."

C. Read the following:

Trends

Are you aware of these positive and negative trends among today's young people? These are some of the negative trends:

(1) Throughout the world, teenagers are using more drugs and narcotics.
(2) Young men and women are committing more acts of vandalism.
(3) Young girls are smoking more cigarettes.
(4) Young people are drinking less coffee.
(5) Both young men and women are rejecting clothes as an indication of status.
(6) Youths are questioning adults' values and priorities.
(7) Students are examining the practical value of conventional education and careers.
(8) The young generation is investigating alternative expressions of religion.
(9) Young people are opposing industries that spoil the environment.

(10)   Young men and women are choosing less traditional lifestyles.

(11)   Many young people are ignoring the differences among social classes, races, and nationalities.

D. Write Away

1.   Rewrite the trends. Tell *what is being done* at the present time.

Your first sentence: **More drugs and narcotics are being used by teenagers throughout the world.**

2.   It is now 50 years later. Rewrite the trends and tell *what was happening*.

Your first sentence: **Throughout the world teenagers were using more drugs and narcotics fifty years ago.**

3.   It is now 50 years later. Rewrite the trends and tell what was *being done*.

Your first sentence: **Fifty years ago, more drugs and narcotics were being used by teenagers throughout the world.**

4.   Rewrite the trends. Include the additional information at the beginning of each sentence.

after **Because**	after **Because of**
In (1), use . . . **feel alienated,**	. . . **feelings of alienation,**

Your first sentences:

1. **Because teenagers feel alienated, they are using more drugs and narcotics.**
2. **Because of teenagers' feelings of alienation, they are using more drugs and narcotics.**

after Because	after Because of
In (2), use . . . **resist authority**	. . . **resistance to authority**
In (3), use . . . **desire to act maturely**	. . . **desires to act maturely**
In (4), use . . . **prefer soft drinks**	. . . **preference for soft drinks**
In (5), use . . . **reject superficial values**	. . . **rejection of superficial values**
In (6), use . . . **differ in outlook**	. . . **difference in outlook**
In (7), use . . . **resent meaningless tradition**	. . . **resentment of meaningless tradition**
In (8), use . . . **disagree with established faiths**	. . . **disagreement with established faiths**
In (9), use . . . **appreciate nature**	. . . **appreciation of nature**
In (10), use . . . **insist on more individual freedom**	. . . **insistence on more individual freedom**
In (11), use . . . **do not accept barriers among people**	. . . **nonacceptance of barriers among people**

E.   Writing Follow-Up

Write your own philosophy. Explain how you feel about
these trends.

_____

_____

_____

_____

_____

_____

_____

_____

Grammatical Index